HRM-Visionarium

The New function of the HR-department: "An eye on the future"

Jon-Arild Johannessen

Copyright © 2016 Author Name

All rights reserved.

ISBN-13:978-1535466776

ISBN-10:1535466774

CONTENTS
PREFACE 5

CHAPTER 1 INTRODUCTION TO THE BOOK 8

INTRODUCTION 8
DEFINITIONS 8
HRM PHILOSOPHY: BACKGROUND AND DEVELOPMENT 9
PROBLEM 11
PROBLEM APPROACH 11
HOW HAS HRM PHILOSOPHY EVOLVED BETWEEN 1980 AND 2016? 12
FUNCTIONAL DIFFERENTIATION AND THE NECESSARY AREAS OF
COMPETENCE 14
WHAT IS THE KNOWLEDGE BASE OF THE NEW HRM PHILOSOPHY? 19

CONCLUSION 28

CHAPTER 2 HOW CAN WE IMPROVE THE EFFECTIVENESS OF HRM STRATEGY? 29

INTRODUCTION 29
DEFINITIONS 29
ISSUE 31
HOW CAN WE UNDERSTAND STRATEGIC HR MANAGEMENT AT
DIFFERENT LEVELS? 32
THE BEHAVIOURAL PERSPECTIVE 36
THE RESOURCE-BASED PERSPECTIVE (RBP) 37
THE KNOWLEDGE-BASED PERSPECTIVE 38
DYNAMIC CAPABILITIES 39
DEVELOPING A TYPOLOGY FOR THE FOUR KNOWLEDGE PERSPECTIVES
ON DIFFERENT LEVELS 40
CONCLUSION 44

CHAPTER 3 VALUE CREATION IN KNOWLEDGE ORGANIZATIONS: ASPECTS OF A THEORY 47

INTRODUCTION 47
INFOSTRUCTURE 57
FRONT LINE FOCUS 62

Modular Flexibility 66
Global Competence Clusters 69
Conclusion 74

CHAPTER 4 PROSPECT THEORY AS AN EXPLANATION FOR RESISTANCE TO ORGANIZATIONAL CHANGE 78

Introduction 78
Decision-making under Uncertainty 81
Framing 88
Heuristic Assessments 92
Specific Measures That Management Can Implement 99
Conclusion 104

CHAPTER 5 KNOWLEDGE MANAGEMENT AND KNOWLEDGE WORKER PERFORMANCE 107

Introduction 107
Historical Context 112
Focus on the Primary Task 117
Practical Tools for the HR Department: Focus on What We Are Supposed To Do 119
Result Orientation 120
Practical Tools for the HR Department: What Can I Contribute That Makes a Difference? 121
Innovation Orientation 124
Practical Tools for the HR Department: How to Design an Organization's Idea-development Processes. 125
Recognition for Knowledge-sharing 126
Practical Tools for the HR-Department: Information Analysis 129
Self-management and Self-organization 130
Practical Tools for the HR-Department: Strengths Analysis 133
Continuous Development of Skills 135
Practical Tools for the HR-Department: Skills and Competence Analysis 140
Conclusion 142

CHAPTER 6 STRATEGIC HRM: A THEORY FOR THE AMBIDEXTROUS ORGANIZATION – A NEW FUNCTION FOR HR DEPARTMENTS   146

INTRODUCTION   146
BRIEF DESCRIPTION OF BEER'S THEORY   152
WHAT ARE THE NEW FUNCTIONS OF HR DEPARTMENTS?   156
THE NEW HR-FUNCTION: "AN EYE ON THE FUTURE"   157
CONCLUSION   165

INDEX   169

CHAPTER ON CONCEPTS   167

REFERENCES   170

ACKNOWLEDGMENTS

We would like to express our thanks to Assistant Professor Siri Hopland, Kristiania University College, Norway, for making the book more reader-friendly than we could have managed ourselves.

Preface

What we examine in this book:

The book discusses the following question: *Which trends will manifest themselves in HR practices in the future?*

The book discusses in detail the following areas of knowledge:

- Knowledge management
- Performance management
- Innovation management
- Change management
- Organizational design.

We examine the following questions:

1. Which key areas of expertise will HR management concentrate on in the future? (Chapter 1).
2. How can organizations maintain their competitive position using strategic HR management? (Chapter 2)
3. What key areas of knowledge will HR management concentrate on in the future? (Chapter 3 – Chapter 5).
4. What new functional areas will HR departments be concerned with in the future? (Chapter 6)

HRM-Visionarium

Chapter 1 Introduction to the book

Introduction

Definitions

In this chapter, the term "HRM philosophy" means the way in which the management of an organization thinks, communicates and acts when using human capital (Ulrich, 2013; 2013a). An organization's "human capital" is the competence (knowledge, skills and attitudes) that promotes the organization's ongoing competitive position (Bohlander et al., 2001). An organization's human capital, rather than its machinery or assets, is its most important resource in the knowledge society (Burton-Jones, 1999). Today, the majority of theorists and practitioners are of the opinion that the people within an organization are its most important resource (Boxall et al., 2007:1-16). Accordingly, the way in which these people are managed is the basis for the organization's success (Pattanayak, 2005:3).

The importance of HRM philosophy is linked to the organization's fundamental values, communications and involvement, including a new psychological contract with the employees focusing on their well-being. The intention was that this should have consequences for the conduct of individual employees (Guest, 2007:128-146).

An explicit HRM philosophy makes it easier for employees to identify and understand the organization's fundamental values, and thereby to create an identity and meaning through their work (Pattanayak, 2005:113).

HRM philosophy: background and development

The starting point for this modern approach to HRM may be found in the work of several authors, but perhaps Fombrun et al. (1984) of Michigan University were among the first to elevate HRM from a purely administrative function to a more strategic role. According to Fombrun et al., HRM should be central to the organization and not simply an administrative function. Fombrun et al. based their HRM cycle on what they identified as the four most important functions of the HR department: recruitment, performance appraisal, rewards, and competence development. At the same time as Fombrun et al. were developing the Michigan model, researchers at Harvard were developing an alternative. The Harvard model encompassed an organization's senior management and a strategic vision for HRM. According to this model, the HR department's autonomous or "stand-alone" activities needed to be integrated to become part of a functioning whole. Thus, since 1984 HRM has had a theoretical foundation.

However, a long time may pass (relatively speaking) from the moment one sees lightning until one hears thunder. In other words, HR is a field that evolves very slowly, as evidenced by the fact that many HR departments continue to operate to this day as if their most important task were personnel administration (Brockbank & Ulrich, 2006:489-504).

Walton (1985) developed the Harvard model further and introduced the concept of reciprocity. The idea was that reciprocity would encourage commitment by employees, which in turn would foster organizational efficiency. Guest (1987; 1989a; 1989b; 1991) also further developed the Harvard model with his four policy goals: strategic integration, a high level of commitment, high quality, and a high degree of flexibility. As mentioned, Story (1989) introduced the concepts of "hard" and "soft" HRM. "Hard" HRM consisted of the quantifiable aspects of HRM, while "soft" HRM related to, for example, motivation, leadership and communication. Legge (1989) introduced the idea that organizational culture was an important aspect of HRM theory and practice.

The classic work on HRM was published for the first time in 1987. Between 1987 and the publication of the ninth edition in 2014, one can see how the field of HRM has evolved (Torrington, et. al., 2014). There are four areas that recur in all nine editions: competence resources, performance, social relations, and remuneration. In general, this is representative of the HRM function viewed from an industrial-society perspective. In the most recent editions (published in the period 2008-2014), however, the authors have addressed the strategic role of the HR department. In any event, the model on which the most widely used book on HRM is based takes as its starting point the HRM philosophy prevalent in industrial societies, where HR departments were seen as units for personnel administration.

Problem

According to Boudreau & Lawler (2009), many HR departments experience problems because they are unable to keep up with the rate of change of the systems they are supposed to support. If this is correct, the consequence is that the HR departments may end up being out of step with the rest of the organization. This is something that often happens, according to Ulrich (2013a: 255). However, businesses, organizations and institutions that manage to accommodate change successfully also have HR departments that manage to be at the forefront of these changes (Ulrich, 2013a: 255).

Problem approach

The principle question this chapter asks is: Which competences will manifest themselves in future HRM philosophy?

The research questions are as follows:

1. How has HRM philosophy evolved between 1980 and 2016?
2. What is the knowledge base of the new HRM philosophy?

Organization

The chapter is organized as follows. Firstly, the historical development of HRM philosophy between 1980 and 2016 will be examined. Secondly, the knowledge base of the new HRM philosophy will be examined. Finally, the areas of competence covered by HRM philosophy towards 2030 will be investigated. In order to come to grips with the possible future developments in HRM philosophy, we have used results and syntheses from trend research. Conceptual generalization is used to create a synthesis and abstraction of HRM philosophy towards 2030 (Johannessen & Adriaenssen, 2016).

How has HRM philosophy evolved between 1980 and 2016?

HRM research may be divided into three sub-groups, which we can term micro-, meso- and macro HRM research.

Micro HRM researches at the level of the individual and the team. It is concerned with recruitment, selection, induction/onboarding, on the job training, development of competence, improving performance and reward systems (Mahoney & Deckop, 1986).

Meso-HRM mainly focuses on the strategic function of HR is an organization. From 1980s onwards, HR departments usually aimed at becoming part of the strategic team in organizations (Walker, 1980). In practice, this meant that HR activities should be linked to strategic thinking (Fombrun et al., 1984). However, it wasn't until the 1990s that this aim became a reality (Ulrich, 1996). Although strategic thinking became part of HR practices, organizations are largely arranged as "silos" filled with their respective functional areas, and have relatively little integration across the organization. In other words, the strategic thinking in HR is to a lesser extent part of the strategic thinking in the other functional "silos" (Wright et al., 2011:2-3).

In the 1980s and 1990s, the importance and prominence of HR's role in organizations increased. The scandals of the early 2000's in several well known companies[1] led to demands for more balanced control mechanisms as an organization principle (Maciariello, 2014:95-103). The financial crisis from autumn 2007 onwards also led to new requirements for HR functions. The reputations of large companies and the financial system itself was now in question, and thus the HR function acquired a new role in, amongst other things,

---

[1] Enron, MCI-WorldCom; Qwest, Adelphia Communications et al.

reputation management and corporate social responsibility (Maciariello, 2014:95). Consequently, it may be said that scandals and the financial crisis resulted in giving chief human resources officers (CHROs) strategically important positions as communication partners with board members (Wright et al., 2011:4).

Macro-HRM focuses on global developments. In an increasingly competitive and global workplace, "the war for talent" became important: how organizations can recruit, cultivate and develop talented employees (Michaels et al., 2001:2). HR departments were given the important strategic task of developing future competence in the company (Ulrich, 2013; 2013a). In essence, this concerned the recruitment and development of knowledge workers whose workplace was the global economy; their task involved operating in close contact with customers and suppliers, which we term here the front line (Michaels et al., 2001:33).

Functional differentiation and the necessary areas of competence

In 1992, Schuler formulated his simple five P model for HRM. The five Ps stand for: "HR-philosophy, HR-policies, HR-programmes, HR-practices and HR-processes" (Schuler, 1992). The model is used often, and is easy to relate to other models. However, it is so general that it resembles perhaps more a framework than a model, and it is difficult to see that it has a theoretical foundation.

Ulrich et al. (2012:19) describe HRM trends over a longer period of time, starting around 1980 when HRM had essentially an administrative role in organizations. The book then reviews and describes the expansion of HRM functions, when HR departments began to go beyond purely administrative functions. The book then shows how HR was incorporated strategically in organizations. Finally, they use the term "HR from the outside in". This, briefly, refers to the fact that HRM philosophy has changed so that developments are brought from the outside world into the company's HR practices. This implies that the HR department takes on an extended responsibility. It may be said that Ulrich et al. (2012) indicate a type of functional differentiation. That is, HRM philosophy has evolved from its administrative and bureaucratic origins to include all the features that companies participate in so as to compete, survive and grow. However, this does not mean that HR departments have to include all the functional areas in an organization; it just means that HR departments should have sufficient variety - the law of requisite variety (Ashby, 1970; 1981) - in order to tackle complexities externally and internally.

HR departments became even more important in the 2000's, because fusions, mergers, bankruptcies, acquisitions and extreme competition in the global economy increasingly brought about a situation whereby organizations needed to have the capability to cope with these processes of change. It was also during this period that there was a growing need for the development of ideas, innovation and management of change processes (Wright et al., 2011: 5). Innovation in small and midsize companies (with no R & D departments) is not the responsibility of any specific department; it is in this context that HR departments may have a new role to play.

In addition to innovation and change processes, the ethical perspective became more prominent in HRM after the turn of the millennium due to the factors mentioned above and developing globalization. This is emphasized by several HRM researchers including Schneider (1987:450), Beer et al. (1984:13), Ulrich (1997:5), Boxall (2007:5), Winstanley and Woodall (2000:6), as well as Grant and Shields (2002).

Before 2000, HR strategy was not geared to monitoring and responding to trends and changes in the outside world; the exception was if these changes directly affected HR. One general example is the production of a company's products in low cost countries, where the HR department would deal with outsourcing and employment processes.

The new HR philosophy that emerged around 2000 (White & Younger, 2013:27-52) dictated that HR departments were given greater responsibility for what may be described using the acronym PESC, which stands for political, economic, social and cultural trends.

Around 2000, organizations and other social systems came to be viewed as being systemically connected: i.e., interconnected and mutually interdependent. This is a view evident in, amongst others, the "Human Resource Competence Study" (White & Younger, 2013:27-52). This global study also shows a change in HR practices - a transition from an administrative focus to a strategic focus, although daily HR administrative processes are maintained. It also shows that HR increasingly needs to access a system that monitors trends in the outside world. HR makes these trends apparent, and shows possible measures that a company's senior management may adopt in order to facilitate the development of sufficient variation in relation to trends in the outside world.

HRM also needs to include the global perspective in their local analyses to a much greater extent. In such a situation, HR departments need to relate the development of individual skills with organizational capabilities (White & Younger, 2013:30).

Many companies have gone through a process from national to international to multinational and now to global. The new feature of global businesses is that they "…share knowledge, talent, capital, customers, and practices around the world. Global firms seek collaborations with networks that take advantage of synergies across borders." (Ulrich, 2013a:256). Interestingly, in this context we find the distinction between multinational and global businesses. Global businesses are strong not because of their size, but rather because of their impact which is due to the fact that they are knowingly connected to other businesses. One of the consequences of such a development is that competition and cooperation are, of necessity, like Siamese twins. In the case of international and multinational businesses, one speaks of lasting competitive advantages whereas in the case of global businesses, lasting cooperative benefits and temporary competitive advantages are more crucial. If this assumption is correct, this will have significant consequences for the development of talented employees and a company's capabilities.

Given the results of Ulrich's research (2013a), HR departments should develop early warning systems that are able to uncover global signals and trends at the earliest possible stage.

Fig. 1 shows the study variables in a PESC window. This chart has been developed by us based on a conceptual generalization of the 25-year empirical research conducted by Ulrich et al. (2013). The PESC window may be used as the basis for the design of an early warning system, monitoring trends and for analysis of an organization's capabilities in relation to developments in the global economy.

Fig. 1 The PESC window as the basis for the development of the necessary competencies in relation to future HRM strategy.

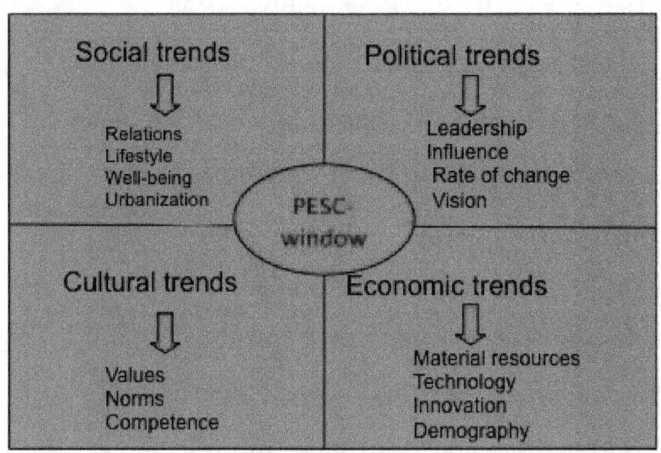

If a distinction is made between tangible and intangible variables then it is clear that most of the variables in the PESC window are intangible, such as leadership, talent and vision (meaning, engagement, commitment). In knowledge organizations, it is estimated that approximately 50% of an organization's market value can be explained by intangible factors (Ulrich & Ulrich, 2010:5). This should provide direction for HRM philosophy, practices and competencies towards 2030.

What is the knowledge base of the new HRM philosophy?

The HR department's main task, say Ulrich et al., is to "create specific and substantial value for customers and shareholders."

(Ulrich et al., 2012:27). This is not a statement based on hope, faith or desire but "…it is a conclusion backed by 25 years of empirical research" (Ulrich et al., 2012:27). Arguably, HRM philosophy should also give employees an answer to the question: Why work for this company? Most people work for more than just money. They work because their job gives them some purpose and is related to specific values. This may be as simple as the importance of relationships with colleagues. It may also concern the identity one creates through work. If the job is meaningful the probability is greater that one develops skills, becomes more committed and dedicated to the job, and contributes more. Correspondingly, this also increases the customers' commitment to the company (Ulrich & Ulrich, 2010:5). Research also shows that when the employee is committed, customers also become committed through this engagement and this ultimately affects the bottom line positively. Ulrich & Ulrich express this as follows: "Making meaning is an important cause and a lead indicator of long-term organizational success" (Ulrich & Ulrich, 2010:5).

In recent years, the HR manager has become one of the most important people in the management teams of several companies (Wright et al., 2011:1). When Jack Welch wrote the book "Winning" he expressed this quite explicitly: "…the head of HR should be the second most important person in any organization" (Welch, 2005:99-100).

From the shadows, from a function that primarily had an

administrative and supervisory role (Walton, 1985:77), HR departments have become more visible and play a completely different role today than twenty or thirty years ago (Wright et al., 2011:1). HRM philosophy has evolved from management and control of the staff to "...commitment; i.e. the strength of an individual's identification with, and involvement in, a particular organization" (Armstrong, 2014a:6). This also agrees with the view of Ulrich & Ulrich (2010:12).

The transition from an HRM philosophy primarily concerned with administrative tasks to one which is more participatory and involved in the organization may be explained in several ways. Recent theories and approaches have provided guidelines for different ways of managing people, for example resource-based theory (Barney & Clark, 2007), institutional theory (Scott, 2013), dynamic capabilities (Helfat et al., 2007) recent theories of knowledge (Polanyi, 1962; 2009; Nonaka & Takeuchi, 1995) recent motivation theories (Asplund, 1970; 2010), new action theories (North, 1990; 1993; 1994; 1996; 1997), prospect theory (Kahneman & Tversky, 2000) and psychological capital (Luthans et al., 2015).

The emergence of globalization and the knowledge society also provides another explanation of this transition in HRM philosophy (Gavin, 2011:29-30). What is new in the knowledge society that indicates a different and more prominent role for the HR departments? The answer to this question falls into at least two main categories.

One major category is related to the new type of employee in the knowledge society: the knowledge worker. Within this category there are at least five types of answers to the question above. Firstly, there is much to suggest that the knowledge worker is motivated by other factors than the industrial worker in the industrial society (Drucker, 1988; 1993; 1999; 1999a). Secondly, we have no clear and explicit answer of how to increase the productivity of knowledge workers, while much knowledge exists concerning the productivity of agriculture and industry workers (Drucker, 1999; 1999a). To increase the productivity of knowledge workers, organizational design, learning systems and reward systems need to be rethought. Thirdly, the infostructure rather than the infrastructure needs to be emphasised, which could have implications for the international workforce. Fourthly, the new information and communication technologies affect where and how people work. Fifthly, the necessity of integrating innovation in all organizations has implications for how one hires, develops, motivates and manages people (Legnick-Hall & Legnick-Hall, 2003).

The other main category is related to the globalization of production, distribution and consumption in the knowledge society. Within this category there are at least two answers. Firstly, at the end of the 20th century and beginning of the 21st century there was an emphasis on the outsourcing of many HR activities.

Among others, this concerned employment-related processes and skills development. The assumption was that external experts could perform various tasks better than the individual HR departments. Secondly, to an increasing extent, the competence that was sought after on the local level could be found in the global competence network. For instance, IT skills that are used on IT projects locally may be accessed in Bangalore, India. When the so-called local competence exists in global competence clusters this entails new requirements for HR departments. One such requirement is cultural understanding, while another is competence regarding interaction and communication in the global space.

It is also possible that new requirements generated by the two main categories of challenges facing HR departments will lead to HR departments being designed and organized differently. In other words, human capital will become more prominent in the knowledge society. Consequently, there is also much evidence that those responsible for managing this capital will need to possess a sufficient variety of skills to cope with variety among the people they manage. This is analogous to Ashby's law of requisite variety (Ashby, 1970; 1981). One consequence of this law is that the HR practices that emerged in the industrial society are no longer adequate in the knowledge society (Legnick-Hall & Legnick-Hall, 2003:xii). This development has a direct impact on the new HRM philosophy. The essence of the new HRM philosophy may be expressed in one sentence: *The way we think will affect the way we act.* This may be explained by two theories, which we will term here Asplund's motivation theory and North's action theory.

Asplund's motivation theory[2] may be briefly described in the following way: *People are motivated by social responses* (Asplund, 2010:221-229). The following statement may be said to be a central point made by Asplund's theory: *When people receive social responses, their level of activity increases.*

Asplund's motivation theory is consistent with North's action theory. North's action theory (North, 1990; 1993; 1994; 1996; 1997) may be expressed in the following statement: *People act on the basis of a system of rewards as expressed in the norms, values, rules and attitudes in the culture (the institutional framework).*

If we link Asplund's motivation theory to North's action theory, we arrive at the following proposition: *People are motivated by the social responses that the institutional framework rewards.* It is this proposition, among other things, that makes it seem reasonable to say that knowledge workers in the global knowledge economy are motivated and act differently than industrial workers in the industrial society. The rationale is that both the social responses and the institutional framework are different in the new emerging knowledge economy than in the hierarchical obedience cultures of the industrial society (Santos & Williamson, 2001:13-55).

---

[2] Asplund's motivation theory, a term we use here, is based on Asplund's research.

On a general level, the background for the new HRM philosophy we see developing may be explained by the great rate of change that globalization and the knowledge society has produced (Ulrich & Ulrich, 2010, preface).

The above description provides a rough sketch of the trends characterising the transition from an industrial society to a knowledge society. HRM philosophy in the knowledge society is mainly oriented towards managing and developing knowledge workers. One of the key factors concerning understanding knowledge workers is how they are motivated and how their productivity can be increased (Drucker, 1999; 1999a). The HR departments that are oriented towards an industrial way of thinking are more concerned with control, recruitment, promotions, competence development, measuring employees' performances, terminating employment and the legal aspects of these processes, etc. Of course, these HRM functions do not disappear in the knowledge society. The point is rather that they are given less focus and become administrative HR activities, while others HR activities take precedence and become more important. The good news in this development, say Ulrich et al. (2008), is that the HR department really plays a crucial role in a fast-changing world. The question that may be asked is: can HR departments contribute to future value creation in businesses? Ulrich et al. (2012) answer this question with an unqualified yes.

Success in the knowledge economy often occurs when an idea is associated with a product or service; in this way, knowledge is applied in practice (Burton-Jones, 1999). If this is correct, it can be imagined that HR departments will take on new functions (Lengnick-Hall & Lengnick-Hall, 2003:18), for instance giving support to knowledge workers so productivity increases.

Another new function is related to the fact that knowledge and specialists are scattered around the world. Consequently, HR departments should ensure that the individual knowledge worker is able to connect to, and build relationships with, global experts and talent wherever it can be accessed (Brockbank, 2013:3-27). This part of the new HR function may be called relationship building aimed at knowledge workers so that they can link up with global competence clusters. Ulrich says the following: "To master HR in today's technologically connected and rapidly changing environment requires insights into global communities" (Ulrich, 2013:v). "Global communities" is here synonymous with our term "global competence clusters". To achieve this, HR departments need to have sufficient variety in their competence. They should be able to understand the global competence clusters, and have insight into social, technological, political and demographic trends. The rationale here is that due to "the war for talent" investors and suppliers are global and no longer local or regional (Ulrich. 2013:vi).

The battle for talent in the new global knowledge economy requires that HR departments focus on the following dual process:

1. Develop talent and organizational capability (what the business is good at and well known for).
2. Connect to talent in the global competence clusters.

Twenty-five years of empirical research shows that the HR departments that manage this double process also contribute significantly to the organization's performance (Brockbank, 2013:8).

A significant innovation in the last 25 years is the development of what we term the infostructure (information structure), as contrasted to the infrastructure. The infostructure is connected to the development of high-speed networks and the consequences that the rapid spread of information has for businesses. Brockbank (2013:8-9) says that the rapid spread of information in the global economy also has consequences for HR departments. HR departments can create value for organizations in the global knowledge economy along the following four axes (Brockbank, 2013:9; Ulrich & Smallwood, 2007):

1. *Global trend analyses*: Design that will be in demand in the future regarding individual talent needs and capabilities of the organization.
2. *Be involved in senior management:* Have a focus on what the organization is designed to do and relate this to the organization's competitive position.

3. *Develop knowledge:* Develop the knowledge that is valued by customers, capital markets, suppliers, partners and public authorities.
4. *Responsibility for innovation and change processes:* When Ulrich et al. (2012:16-17) suggest new roles for HR departments, this focuses on "driving innovation (and) managing organizational change", amongst others. The HR department's role in innovation processes is also underlined by Zhou et al. (2013), and Pattanayak (2005:8-11).

Conclusion

The problem approach in this chapter is: Which competences will be manifested in the HRM philosophy of the future?

The specific answer to this question is given along the following two axes. Firstly, there are the necessary areas of competence. Secondly, there are the sufficient areas of competence. The necessary and sufficient areas of competence are shown in Fig. 2.

Fig. 2. The necessary and sufficient areas of competence for strategic HRM towards 2030.

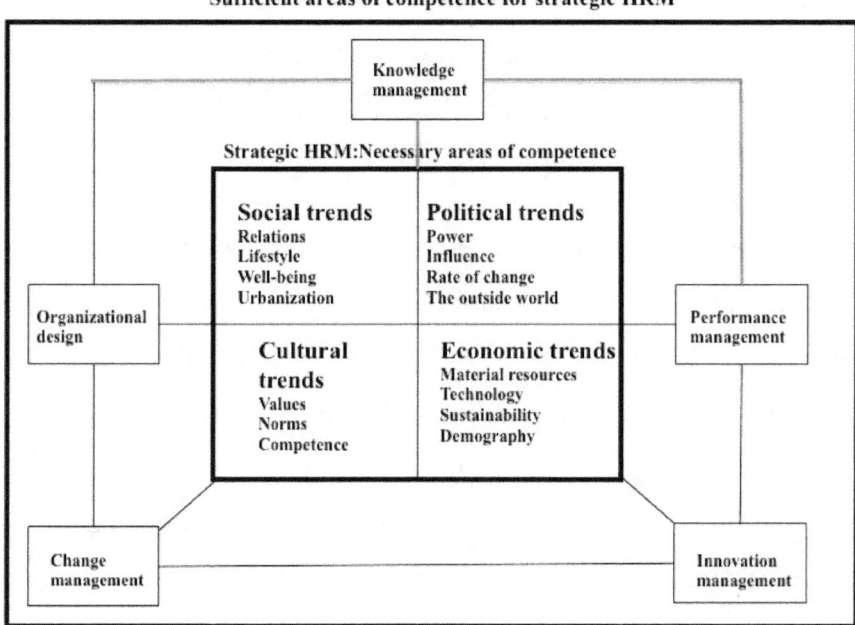

Chapter 2 How can we improve the effectiveness of HRM strategy?

Introduction

Definitions

HR management is defined here as the various HR practices at different levels (micro, meso, macro) used for the purposes of managing people within organizations.

Here we consider HR management as the aggregate of the functions performed by an HR department, or to quote Wright & McMahan (2001:298): "It is the sum of the technical knowledge within each of these functions that we refer to as the field of HRM."

Strategic HR management is defined here as *the choices an HR department makes with regard to human resources for the purposes of achieving the organization's goals.* This is analogous to the view of Storey et al. (2009:3) and consistent with the definition we employ of HR management. This means that strategic HR management must be focused on the micro, meso and macro-levels. There are many definitions of strategic HR management. Some are mentioned below: "use of human resources in order to achieve lasting competitive advantages for the business" (Mathis and Jackson, 2008:36); "management of the employees, expressed through management philosophy, policy and praxis" (Torrington et al., 2005:28); "development of a consistent practices in order to support the strategic goals of the business" (Mello, 2006:152); "a complex system with the following characteristics: vertical integration, horizontal integration, efficiency, partnership" (Schuler and Jackson, 2005).

Issue

The problem we take as our starting point is the confirmed gap in strategic HR management between theory and practice (Rynes, 2007:985; Uysal, 2014). HR managers find it difficult to describe how HR practices promote value creation. Some links were described, however, in studies dating from the 1990s, when the concept of strategic HR management was first developed. Huselid's classic study published in 1995 shows a statistical link between HR practices in relation to "turnover" and profit and market value. Since Huselid's study was published, many studies have demonstrated similar links between HR practices and various markers of organizational performance. The problem however is that none of these studies have been based on clearly defined structures, or on a clear knowledge base. This makes accumulating knowledge difficult, and to a large extent we are forced to return to Huselid's 1995 starting point in order to demonstrate the existence of such links. Accordingly, this area of research has been characterized by fragmentation, both in relation to levels (micro, meso, macro) and the knowledge base that has been applied. This is also the core of the problem that we will attempt to address in this chapter.

Research questions:

1. How can we understand strategic HR management at different levels?
2. What knowledge base do we have for strategic HR management?

Organization

We have organized the chapter in relation to the two research questions.

How can we understand strategic HR management at different levels?

Through a literature review of strategic HR management, Wright and Boswell (2002) found that research had focused on single or multiple HR practices in order to discover the relationship between HR practices and organizational performance. In addition, the various studies were spread across various levels, i.e. individual level (micro) as well as group and organizational levels (meso). Wright and Nishii (2013:99) say the following about the research at the various levels: "To date SHRM researchers have focused on examining true variance at the organizational level, with relatively less attention being paid to variance at other levels of analysis."

Storey et al. (2009:4-5) indicate three levels in strategic HR management: the individual level, or micro; the organizational level, or meso; the external level, or macro. These three levels can be further divided in different ways. To avoid confusion, it is important to be explicit concerning which level is being discussed; however, it must also be kept in mind that strategies adopted at one level can affect one or more of the other levels. This relationship can be shown in a Boudon-Coleman diagram, which was developed by Bunge (1998: 76-79) on the basis of insights made by the sociologists Boudon and Coleman. The purpose of the diagram is to show the relationship between the different levels, such as the macro and micro-levels. For instance, changes at the macro-level, such as technological innovations, can lead to increased income at the micro-level.

An important purpose of the diagram is to identify which processes maintain or change the phenomenon or problem under investigation. The Boudon-Coleman diagram represents a "mixed strategy" (Bunge, 1998:78), which Bunge uses in his research. Bunge states: *"When studying systems of any kind a) reduce them to their components (at some level) and the interaction among these, as well as among them and environmental items - but acknowledge and explain emergence³ whenever it occurs: and b) approach systems from all pertinent sides and on all relevant levels, integrating theories or even research fields whenever unidisciplinarity proves to be insufficient"* (Ibid). The purpose of this research strategy is to arrive at a deeper and more complete explanation of behaviour in social systems at various levels. This also applies to research related to strategic HR management.

A figurative representation of the Boudon-Coleman diagram, as well as the different levels is shown in Fig. 1.

---

[3] An emergent is if something new occurs on one level that has not previously existed on the level below. By emergent we mean here: "Let S be a system with composition A, i.e. the various components in addition to the way they are composed. If P is a property of S, P is emergent with regard to A, if and only if no components in A possess P; otherwise P is to be regarded as a resulting property with regards to A"(Bunge, 1977:97).

Fig. 1. Strategic HR management – an analytical framework

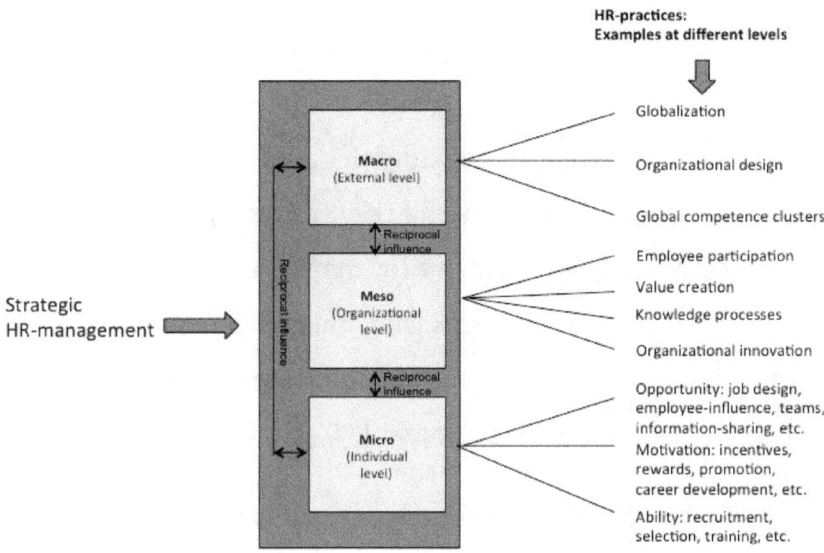

What knowledge base do we have for strategic HR management?

We will very shortly describe the following perspectives: behavioural; resource-based; knowledge-based; and dynamic capabilities. These perspectives are chosen because together they cover the micro, meso and macro-levels, and because these four knowledge bases are consistent with HR management issues in the knowledge society we see emerging (White and Younger, 2013; Ulrich, 2013a).

Finally, we will develop a typology that integrates the various knowledge perspectives and different levels (micro, meso, macro).

The behavioural perspective

In this perspective, we are concerned with roles and behaviour (Jackson et al., 1989; Becker and Huselid, 1998). One focuses less on employees' knowledge, skills and proficiency (Wright and McMahan, 1992: 305). The main focus is on internal conditions, even if one does not ignore the influence of the external world on the achievement of objectives (Schuler and Jackson, 1987).

The purpose of the various HR practices in this perspective is to influence and shape employees' attitudes and behaviour. The most effective attitudes and behaviour will be context and situation dependent. In this perspective, strategic HR management should aim to utilise those HR practices that most effectively contribute to realising organizational objectives.

Concerning the relationship between HR management and strategy, Wright and McMahan (1992: 303-304) say the best model is possibly Schuler and Jackson's (1987), which takes as its starting point Porter's competitive strategy model (Porter, 1980). Schuler and Jackson's model was used to discuss how to develop innovation, promote quality processes and reduce costs in organizations.

The resource-based perspective (RBP)

The resource-based perspective is the most commonly used theoretical framework when researching HR management and strategic HR management, say Boxall and Purcell (2008), Paauwe, et al., (2013: 5) and Delery and Shaw (2001), inter alia. The perspective has been particularly important when attempting to explain the relationship between strategic HR management and organizational performance (Wright, et al., 2001). The emphasis on internal resources, which this perspective focuses on, legitimizes the idea that human resources are crucial for an organization's competitive position (Wright, et al., 2001: 702).

However, it is argued that only those individuals who possess core competencies of the organization are of crucial importance for the organization's competitive position (Lepak and Snell, 1999). If we assume that core competencies are the most crucial resource for businesses, then the development and application of this resource will be of particular importance. Logically, this will relate to the importance of an organization's ability to learn more quickly and efficiently than the competition (Boxall, 1996: 65). Core competencies are, as a rule, related to the core processes in an enterprise, i.e. the activities the organization is designed to do. It is thus the emphasis on human resources related to core competencies that links strategic HR management to a focus on core processes and competencies (Ulrich, 1991; Ukrich &

Brockbank, 2005).

The knowledge-based perspective

The knowledge-based perspective is defined here as creating, expanding and modifying internal and external competencies to promote what the organization is designed to do (Grant, 2003: 203).

It was Grant (1991;1996) who conceptualized the knowledge-based perspective. Grant considered an organization a place where knowledge was integrated and used for a specific purpose. According to Grant, it is individuals who develop knowledge while the organization integrates this knowledge and applies it in order to reach certain goals. Therefore, we say that this perspective relates to both micro and meso-levels.

From the late 1990s onwards, many researchers emphasise the importance of knowledge, regarding it as the most essential resource of businesses (Grant, 2000; 2012). They take the resource-based perspective as their starting point, but focus specifically on the different types of knowledge as drivers of how organizations can maintain and improve their competitive position (Barney, 1991; 1995;2001; Grant, 1991; Nonaka and Takeuchi, 1995; 2002).

Dynamic capabilities

Dynamic capabilities stem from the resource-based perspective and evolutionary thinking in strategy literature (Teece, 2011; 2013: 3-65; 82-113; Nelson and Winter, 1982). The dynamic perspective attempts to explain what promotes an organization's competitive position over time, through innovation and growth (Teece, 2013: x).

The original thinking concerning dynamic capabilities may be related to Teece et al. (1997). These authors defined dynamic capabilities as an organization's ability to create, develop and modify its internal and external expertise in order to address changes in the external world.

Later works expanded the concept of dynamic capabilities to include an organization's ability to create changes in the market (Eisenhardt and Martin, 2000; Teece, et.al., 2002). The modification of the original definition has involved a greater emphasis on resources other than expertise, which Teece et al. (1997) initially focused on. Whatever the development of dynamic capabilities, both Helfat et al. (2007) and Teece (2013: ix) say that the basis of the perspective rests on tacit knowledge, organizational processes and senior management skills. This links dynamic capabilities closely to the knowledge-based perspective. The difference here is that the knowledge-based perspective focuses on the micro and meso levels while dynamic capabilities has its main focus on the meso and macro levels.

Dynamic capabilities focus not only on resources within an organization, but also the resources an organization controls and is dependent on in the external world. The word dynamic refers to the fact that an organization repeats activities and processes in a pattern or routine and not only as an ad-hoc activity (Helfat et al., 2007: 5).

Developing a typology for the four knowledge perspectives on different levels

After this review of the knowledge base of strategic HR management, we have developed the following typology that integrates the various knowledge perspectives in relation to the different levels.

Fig. 2. The knowledge base and levels of strategic HR management: A typology

	Internal	Internal-external
Meso/macro	**The resource-based perspective** — focus on Necessary and sufficient resources	**Dynamic capabilities** — focus on Contextual understanding
Micro/meso	**The behavioural-Theory perspective** — focus on Cause and effect understanding	**The knowledge-based perspective** — focus on Tangible and intangible processes

Level

Main focus

Analysis and implications

It seems reasonable to assume that strategic HR management has garnered much attention because it has the potential to change how one thinks about organizations (Wayne, 2015). There is an assumption that if organizations are to survive in the global knowledge economy, then thinking about HR management must move more towards the organizational (meso) and external (macro) levels, rather than continuing to focus so strongly on the individual (micro) level, as HR management has tended to until now (Darwish, 2013: 1). This assumption has focused attention on the link between HR management and organizational performance (Bratton and Gold, 2012: 50). Two historical perspectives have dominated attempts to understand this link: system theory and the strategic perspective (Darwish, 2013: 1). Today the dominant perspective is one that takes a more integrated approach, involving the application of knowledge from various different perspectives (Storey et al., 2009: 4-6; Truss, et al., 2012: 139-159; Combs et al., 2006; Jiang et al., 2012).

Several empirical investigations have attempted to demonstrate a link between HR practices and organizational performance (Huselid, 1995; Delery and Dorty, 1996; Guthrie, 2000). Researchers have also attempted to understand the mechanism or drivers underlying such a link (Wright et al., 2005). Bowen and Ostroff (2004) have developed a model to demonstrate the link. Their conclusions, which are founded in communications theory, are that different HR practices indicate to employees how they should react in different situations.

Early research in the United States into the link between strategic HR management and organizational results was ambiguous (Wright and Snell, 1998; Welbourne and Cyr, 1999). Research is ongoing, however, into the link between strategic HR management and organizational performance (Storey et al., 2009:4-6; Truss et al., 2012:139-159). Today, one can say that there is confirmed evidence of a link between strategic HR management and various organizational results (Combs et al., 2006; Jiang et al., 2012). However, we know little about the social mechanisms, or drivers, that may explain this link.

If we clarify the theoretical basis for research on strategic HR management, we can map out the various findings in a more orderly manner. This mapping can provide us with insight into which HR practices lead to which results. The practice that exists makes it almost impossible to explain the empirical findings of research on strategic HR management (Mabey et al., 2002). Mabey et al. express this in the following way: "This is why it is so hard (in fact impossible) to obtain agreement on what SHRM really is; and this is why we find such a strange confusion and medley of different sorts of writings with different sorts of approaches and agenda" (Mabey et al., 2002: 6).

The research model we have developed in response to Mabey's statement, and which is developed on the basis of this chapter, is shown in Fig. 3. Fig. 3 incorporates the various levels shown in Fig. 1 and the knowledge bases shown in Fig. 2.

Fig. 3. A model for future research into strategic HR management

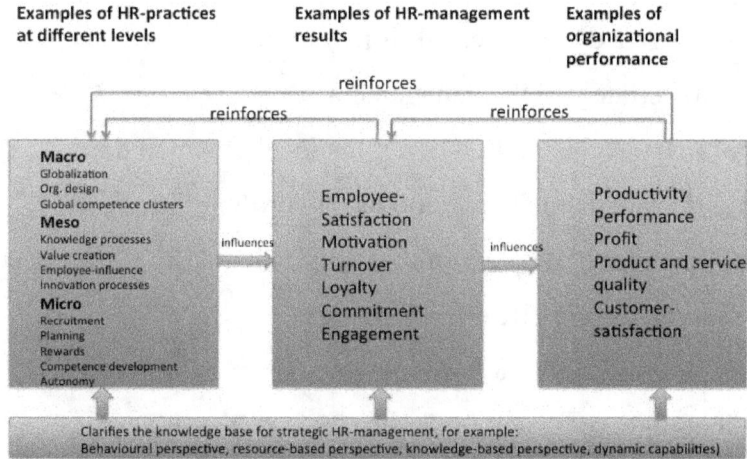

What we have done is propose a framework both for different knowledge bases (Fig. 2) and for different levels for research and the implementation of strategy (Fig. 1). This is integrated in Fig. 3, which shows the suggested analytical research model.

Conclusion

The problem for discussion in this chapter was: *How can organizations maintain their competitive position with the help of strategic HR management?*

The short answer to this question is as follows:

1. Organizations must be explicit as to what theoretical perspective or perspectives are being applied (behavioural perspective; resource-based perspective; a knowledge-based perspective; dynamic capabilities) when implementing strategic HR management.
2. Organizations must be explicit about the level at which this theoretical perspective is being applied (micro/individual, meso/organizational, meta/external world) when implementing strategic HR management.
3. The effective implementation of strategic HR management is dependent upon organizational awareness of the links

between HR practices at different levels, the desired results of HR management, and the desired level of organizational performance.

Suggestions for further research

Empirical research has attempted to find how variations in the use of different HR practices in different organizations influence variations in organizational performance. In contrast, there has been little research into this link within individual organizations. There has been an assumption that HR practices are similar within individual organizations. In order to gain greater understanding of how HR practices affect performance within an individual organization, we wish to obtain a different kind of knowledge by focusing on longitudinal case studies. The assumption here is that one may well imagine people will react differently to similar HR practices. If this assumption is correct, HR practices will be benefited by research that is designed with aims other than identifying variations between organizations.

Variation between different organizations also tells us nothing about the social mechanisms or drivers behind the link between HR practices and performance. In order for the explanation of any variation to have practical relevance, it is important to understand the social mechanisms at work. In order to generate knowledge about the social mechanisms, it is important not to conflate different levels of logic (micro, meso, macro), and also different knowledge perspectives (e.g., behavioural perspective; resource-based perspective; a knowledge-based perspective; dynamic capabilities). If research is not consistent in these two areas, ultimately one will simply be left with a great deal of knowledge about variations between HR practices and organizational performance. HR practices will gain little from this knowledge, however, because we will have failed to identify the social mechanisms that explain the links.

Against this background, we propose the following research design:

1. It is necessary to develop a larger meta-analysis that addresses the distinctions between the different levels (micro, meso, macro) and theoretical perspectives applied in the research (behavioural perspective, resource-based perspective, a knowledge-based perspective, dynamic capabilities). This may clarify what findings exist within different knowledge perspectives and different levels. In this way, we may come closer to evidence-based research into strategic HR management.
2. It will be important to focus on the social mechanisms that may explain the links found in empirical research. If we fail to do this, we will simply be gathering a mass of data

about variations, without being able to suggest what HR practices should do to promote performance and how this will occur.

3. More research into the link between different HR practices and performance within individual organizations will also be necessary in order to increase our knowledge base about ways in which strategic HR management can contribute to improving an organization's competitive position.

Chapter 3 Value creation in knowledge organizations: Aspects of a theory

Introduction

The term "knowledge-based organizations" is used here to mean an organization that is "composed largely of specialists who direct and discipline their own performance through organized feedback from colleagues, customers, and headquarters" (Drucker, 1988: 3). Such an organization "is structured around information, not hierarchy"(Maciarello, 2014:71). As far as we are aware, the term "knowledge worker" was used by Drucker first in 1959 (Drucker, 1959:122). Berger provides a definition of "knowledge worker" that gives the term the same meaning as ascribed to it by Drucker and Maciarello; that is, that knowledge workers are "people whose occupations deal with the production and distribution of symbolic knowledge"(Berger, 1987:66).

There are many examples of knowledge-based organizations: modern hospitals, symphony orchestras, universities, consultancies, engineering firms, architectural practices, etc.

The main function of a manager in a knowledge-based organization is to coordinate the flow of information between experts, and to ensure efficiency in work processes targeted at customers, users, patients etc. (Maciarello, 2014:71). A manager in such an organization does not need to possess an expert's highly specialized knowledge, but he or she must be able to communicate with experts using their professional language (Bohlander et al., 2001). In order to do this, a manager must possess contextual confidence. The manager does not need to have the same level of competence as the people he or she will manage, but he or she must have an understanding of, and be intimately acquainted with, the context (Vallima & Hoffman, 2008). Contextual confidence will enable the manager to ensure that the intended function of the system is implemented: that the organization's primary tasks are coordinated and implemented with maximum efficiency, and that everyone's capacity to perform is exploited to the full (Beer, 1995).

In addition, a manager in a knowledge-based organization must have the ability to analyse such information as is necessary for the organization to perform. He or she must also be able to communicate this information to employees (Brockbank & Ulrich, 2006).

The knowledge workers must understand what is being communicated so that they can act in the light of this information (Maciarello, 2014:72). Drucker emphasizes the point that it is necessary to have the ability to communicate information to those who will be able to apply it most appropriately and productively (Drucker, 1999; 1999a). The point of contextual confidence is that it will enable the manager to communicate appropriate information in an understandable manner. Otherwise, while the information may be completely correct, it may be completely useless for the recipient.

Early in this debate, Savage (1995) pointed out that the advent of the knowledge society was an event equivalent to the advent of the agricultural society, or the industrial society. In the knowledge society, information will be capable of rapid transformation into resources that can by applied for value creation (Castelfranchi, 2007). The knowledge society is dependent on the existence of new technology, both ICT and the internet (Vallima & Hoffman, 2008; UNESCO, 2005). While information may be transformed into knowledge that may be used in value-creation processes, it is also true that knowledge not applied in a process that is subject to reflection and critical thinking may be counterproductive for value creation (Innerarity, 2012). A key characteristic of the knowledge society is the status of knowledge as the central commodity that is exchanged for economic prosperity. Just as agricultural goods were the key characteristic of the agricultural society, and industrial goods the key characteristic of the industrial society, so is knowledge the primary commodity of the knowledge society (Burton-Jones, 1999). Accordingly, the knowledge worker is the main class of worker in the knowledge society, just as the industrial worker was in the industrial society and the agricultural worker in the agricultural society (Drucker, 1969; 1988; 1993; 1999; 1999a).

As knowledge becomes the most important value-creation factor in the knowledge economy, there is also growing criticism of the prioritization of knowledge (Gross, 2010). There was similar criticism, however, during the transition from the agricultural society to the industrial society, when those who felt their position was under threat took to destroying industrial machines (Bowden, 1965:73). It is reasonable to anticipate that people who feel themselves threatened by the knowledge society are those who do not have the same access to knowledge processes and feel they are being marginalized (Sennet, 1998; 2013). These people will probably counteract, ignore and minimize the significance of knowledge (Guest, 2007).

The global knowledge economy is a result of globalization

(Hamel, 2012). Globalization has many different aspects. One is an expansion of the concept of free trade (Santos & Williamson, 2001). Another is the emergence of new spheres of knowledge (Ulrich, 2013). One way of looking at the expansion of free trade and the development of new knowledge is to consider our analytical models, which are based on the concept of the nation state, as undergoing change (see Bauman, 1992:65).

One view proposed by Marr (1995), which concerns the development of globalization and knowledge enterprises, is that the deregulation of the money market during the 1980s accelerated globalization because it put an end to national autonomy. Hirst (1993) and Hutton (1995) take a different view. They see the expanding market as an important driving force in the development of globalization. Another way of looking at growing globalization is to consider China opening up to foreign capital at the end of the 20th century and the fall of the Berlin Wall in 1989. As a result of these two events, approximately 1.5 billion people entered the capitalist market.

What is new about the knowledge society, in our understanding, is that production has moved from classical industrial production in the industrial society to high-technology production based on new knowledge resources, new organizational methods and new technologies in the knowledge society (White & Younger, 2013). The new knowledge workers are those who, among other things, add content to what many of us access on a daily basis in the form of knowledge resources on the internet. In Europe alone, these people comprise approximately seven million knowledge workers (Jemielniak, 2012; UNESCO, 2005). These are knowledge workers who value creative processes and who are result-oriented (Drucker, 1999a).

Unlike industrial workers, knowledge workers do not appear to identify themselves with other knowledge workers as a collective phenomenon (Sennet, 1998; 2004; 2006). They identify with their own results, opportunities and expectations, not unlike an entrepreneur or an owner of capital (see Thurow, 1999).

In the industrial society, the infrastructure emerged as a crucial factor in value creation, and included the transport of goods and energy. In the knowledge society, there is much to suggest that it is the information structure, hereafter referred to as the *infostructure*, which will be a crucial factor in value creation.

The infostructure is important for information, communications and knowledge processes, as well as for "connectance" in large dynamic systems (Ashby, 1970). Amongst other things, the infostructure enables distances and borders to be reduced and diminished. This applies to geographical, psychological, cultural and social distances and borders (Baird & Henderson, 2001).

Consequently, the infostructure directly affects transactions in and across different organizations (Williamson, 2013). The development of the infostructure affects the arranging of activities within and between organizations (Boxall & Purcell, 2010).

James G. Miller (1978) was one of the first to develop a theory for infostructures in social systems. Together with his research team, he examined eleven information processes (infostructure) in a social system, which we have tried to illustrate here using symbols in Fig. 2.

In addition to the infostructure, what we term the front line (i.e. those who are in contact with customers, users, citizens, patients, students, etc.) will have greater significance for value creation in individual businesses (Hannah et al., 2015). The rationale is that customers have increased competence and expect to meet someone who has equal or equivalent competence (Drucker, 1999; 1999a). Another reason is related to the fact that customers and suppliers will increasingly participate in innovation processes, more so than previously (Ramaswamy & Ozcan, 2014).

In order for the front line to be an important factor for value creation in an individual business, it is crucial that it is designed to identify and use signals and information that can be used for creativity, innovation and continuous quality improvement of the business's products and services (Jemielniak, 2012).

Creative processes are driven by competition in the global

economy, where visions and expectations aimed at creating that which is new are important for value creation (Hamel, 2002; 2012); consequently, social systems will be greatly changed (Sennet, 1998; 2013). Social earthquakes will occur at both the local level of the individual, and globally for larger groups of people (see Luttwak, 1999; Sennet, 1998). Cost pressures and extreme competition will lead to a fragmentation of work processes (Hannah et al., 2015; Albrow, 1999). This fragmentation reflects an extreme specialization, which we here term a modulization of work processes (Garud et.al., 2002). This is the result of work processes being distributed, changes in organizational boundaries and the use of global partners and contractors (Drucker, 1988). The modulization of work processes increases the focus on global competence networks (Michaels et al., 2001), resulting in the manufacture of products using global rather than local expertise. These global competence networks are important for value creation in the new knowledge economy (Ramaswamy & Ozcan, 2014). Underlying factors for global competence networks are increased individualization and de-emphasising collective solutions (Sennett, 1998; 2004).

Competence in the knowledge society is a significant factor in the production process (see Boisot, 1998). It is largely rooted in global networks (see Shapiro & Varian, 1999), where extreme global specialization, focusing on core processes and competencies, is emphasised to a greater extent than previously (Tapscot &

Williams, 2006). Control of development, exchange and integration of knowledge is therefore a central management mechanism for value creation processes in knowledge-based organizations (Santor & Williamson, 2001). This also implies a transition from Porter's focus on industrial clusters (Porter, 2004) to a greater emphasis on global competence networks and clusters. These global competence networks will be geographically anchored at various places around the world but are connected and integrated by new technology (Mongkhonvanit, 2010:1950). The global clusters of competence seem to direct attention towards the productivity of knowledge workers, because it is they who are responsible for most of the value creation in global knowledge businesses. In this context, identity seems to veer away from the collective towards the development of the individual knowledge worker's expertise and their own motives and needs (Drucker, 1999; 1999a). In such a situation, social contracts based on the responsibility of the collective become less prominent (Sennet, 1998; 2004; 2006; 2013). This development leads to an increased focus on the productivity of knowledge workers (Drucker, 1999; 1999a), which, it seems reasonable to assume, will lead to further modulization of economic activities and processes, and promote individual solutions at the expense of collective ones (Pyöriä, 2005). Although the focus turns more toward the individual, it is not necessarily the case that this will lead to increased respect, responsibility and dignity of the individual (Sennett, 2004).

Our understanding of globalization and the knowledge society is that they are a natural continuation of the industrial society. The new knowledge society involves new technology, new ways of organizing, new global competence clusters, and new knowledge workers who were not visible to the same extent in the industrial society. In other words, we view the knowledge society as a natural continuation of the modern society rather than a postmodern construction, which agrees with Bauman's view (Bauman, 2011).

Our fundamental assumption, which we have presented in the introduction, is that the interaction between the four elements of infostructure, front line focus, modular flexibility, and global clusters of competence, promote value creation processes in knowledge-based organizations.

The phenomenon we examine here is the transition from the industrial society to a society increasingly based on knowledge resources. The question we ask is: What are the key value creation processes in a knowledge-based organization? The first aim is to understand and explain the social mechanisms and the related social processes that influence the development of knowledge-based organizations. The second aim is to investigate what implications this development will have for management roles in the future.

Fig. 1 summarizes the introduction, and shows how the chapter is organized.

Fig. 1: Key value creation processes in the knowledge economy.

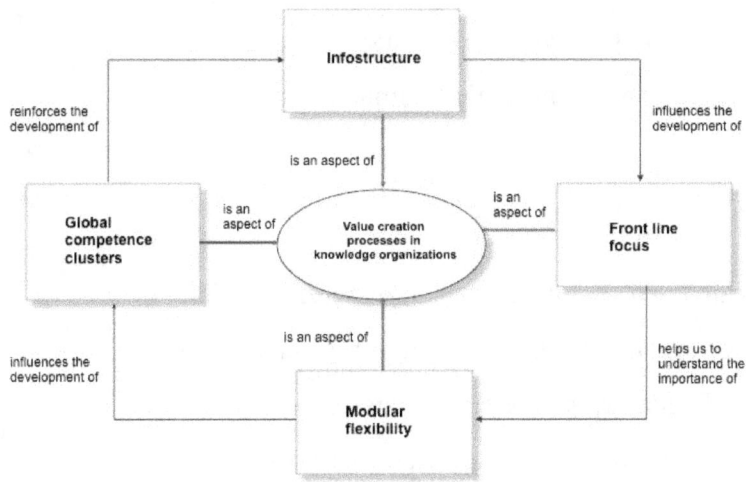

Infostructure

The infostructure concerns the processes that enable the development, transfer, analysis, storage, coordination and management of data, information and knowledge. The infostructure consists of eleven generic processes, as shown in Fig. 2 (Miller, 1978).

The infostructure forms the basis for communication processes and the development of knowledge. It is also highly instrumental in establishing new networks on a global scale (Baird & Henderson, 2001). It is precisely the development of the new infostructure that enables new global cooperation networks as well as new organizational and leadership forms (Tapscott & Williams, 2006). While the infrastructure facilitates the transport of goods, services and energy, the infostructure coordinates and integrates information resources on a large scale (Ramaswamy & Ozcan, 2014).

The eleven processes in the infostructure may be considered as nodes in a social network at different levels, for example team, organization, society, and region, all in the global space. Together, the eleven processes comprise the totality of the infostructure (Haag et al., 2012). The purpose of the nodes is to coordinate information so that social interaction is facilitated and new knowledge developed. The idea is that when the nodes in such a social global network co-create new knowledge and innovation is developed (Hamel, 2012).

The assumption is that in the transition from an industrial to a knowledge economy, the centre of gravity for employment shifts (Tapscot & Williams, 2006). In the knowledge society, knowledge workers perform specialized functions related to the eleven information processes in the infostructure (Reinhart et. al., 2011). Specialization within each of the eleven information processes leads to the production of knowledge in cooperating global competence clusters (Garud & Langlois, 2002).

Each of these eleven infostructure processes is strategically important for knowledge-based organizations (Castelfranchi, 2007). Dominance of one or more of these processes allows for the possibility of control over value creation in the knowledge society (Hamel, 2012). Through control of individual processes, one has the opportunity to influence activities in other processes (Davenport, 2005). The various processes have their relative importance for value creation in the various social systems (Boisot, 1998). At the same time, they have different emphasis depending on the level that is being focused on.

Proposition 1: In the knowledge organization there will be a change in emphasis from infrastructure to the infostructure.

Management implications: The greater the emphasis on the infostructure in relation to skills development and employment, the more incomprehensible changes will seem in the social systems to those exposed to these changes, as well as the change of functional areas and competence.

Social implications: The development of the infostructure

may be understood as a systemic and radical innovation. It is radical because it has serious consequences for so many people around the globe. It affects almost every individual's working and private life. It is systemic because it is interconnected at many different levels, and changes in one place will affect change processes elsewhere because there is a large degree of "connectance" (Ashby, 1970).

Fig. 2 shows a schematic diagram of the infostructure processes. These processes relate to Miller (1978), but are conceptualized by us.

Fig. 2. Infostructure processes

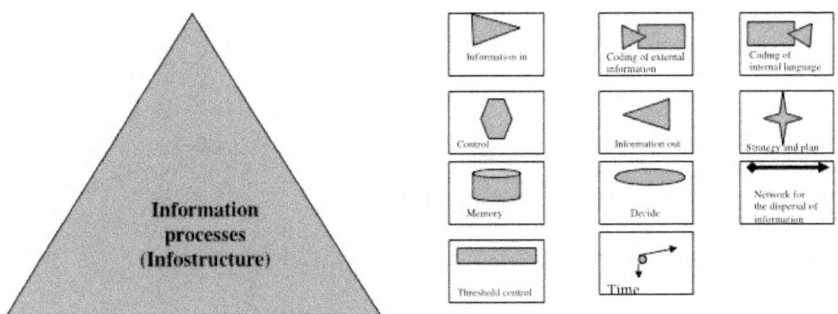

An example of a system that has been especially affected by the change in emphasis from infrastructure to the infostructure is the postal service in various countries. As the emphasis in social development began to emphasize the infostructure with a relative de-emphasis of the infrastructure, parts of the postal functions were taken over by other information carriers. An example of this is email in various networking solutions, which is represented in Fig. 2 by the symbol *network for the dispersal of information*. The consequences of this for postal services have included both the closure of post offices and the dismissal of many employees, as well as the change of functional areas and competence. The main development was a greater emphasis on various information processes as shown schematically in Fig. 2.

How the knowledge society develops is not immediately apparent, because its production processes do not follow the logic of the industrial society (Hamel, 2012; Tapscott & Williams, 2006). The production logic of the industrial society is being replaced by the new and different production logic of the knowledge society. The new logic is created by creative production on the internet, an extreme focus on innovation, and a situation where global competence clusters replace local industrial clusters (Tapscott & Williams, 2006; Thurow, 1999). One of the consequences is a stronger focus on the infostructure, and thereby a decrease in the industrial production logic framed by among others Michael Porter (Porter, 1998; 2004).

Where one is placed within the infostructure is important with regard to the impact and influence one has within the organization. This position, coupled to the goals of the organization, i.e. what it is designed to do (Beer, 1995), is decisive for determining the influence one has within the organization (Innerarity, 2012).

When the competence of customers increases, it is reasonable to assume that they expect to meet high levels of competence in their dealings with the organization. This can lead to a shift of focus in the organization logic of knowledge-based organizations, from hierarchical positions to the front line. The front line in organizations consists of those people who are in close contact with customers, users, suppliers etc. (Jemielniak, 2012). If this assumption is correct, the development of both the infostructure and focus on the front line will lead to major consequences for the role of management in the future.

Front line focus

If it is correct that information and communication processes are essential for value creation in the knowledge society, which Reinhart et al. (2011) claim, competence in the front line will be crucial for efficient organizations. It is in dealings with customers that these processes can culminate in that which is creatively new, and where knowledge is transformed into value creation for the customer (Hamel, 2012). This can also be derived from both theory and practice related to open innovation processes (Chesbrough et al., 2008). The rationale is that the competent customer will prefer the competent supplier (Prahalad & Krishnan, 2008). A necessary condition to achieve this is that the bureaucratic structures are deconstructed, and competence, service, information and decisions are moved to the front line (Hannah et al., 2015). If this doesn't occur, it could hinder restructuring and be a costly element of knowledge-based organizations (Jemielniak, 2012).

Creativity and innovation are prerequisites for value creation in the knowledge society (Prahalad & Krishnan, 2008; Hamel, 2012). Bureaucracy, with its stabilizing thought mode, has difficulty in adapting to rapid changes because change dynamics are not bureaucracy's primary thought mode (Bauman, 2011).

The bureaucratic model was effective for its time, where stability was the primary focus. In the knowledge society, however, change processes are the primary mode because globalization, rapidity of information processes, focus on innovation, and the rapid spread of innovation lead to dynamic change processes (Prahalad & Krishnan, 2008). Creative destruction will probably be normal in such a situation because the pace of change increases in the global knowledge economy (Hamel, 2012). This could lead to demand for major reorganization and increasing pace of change in the industrial society (Rooney et al., 2008: 55-57; 160-161).

A common feature of the knowledge society seems to crystallize as structural links, or "connectance" in Ashby's model (Ashby,

1970). It seems possible that continuous changes in structural connections will lead to customers' expectations, wants and needs changing (Ramaswamy & Ozcan, 2014). Coping with these continuous changes presupposes that organizations have sufficient variety in their capabilities so that they can match customers' competencies, which is related to the "law of requisite variety" (Ashby, 1970). It is reasonable to assume that the capability must exist where the customer interacts with the business - in the front line. Sufficient competence in the front line, satisfying customers' requirements, will be a decisive competitive factor for businesses (Nordhaug, 1994). If competence in the front line is crucial, and the front line is largely identical with where decisions are taken, perhaps bureaucratic structures will be less important for decision-making processes in knowledge based organizations (Davenport, 2005).

Competence in the front line, collective learning structures between businesses, customers and suppliers, and flexibility as a structuring mode will in such an organization be key creation processes (Hannah et al., 2015).

Requisite variety in competence, in relation to the individual customer, presupposes an information system in the front line that focuses on continuous change in the customer's needs and wants. In addition, the organization will have a competitive advantage when they have an organizational learning system that focuses on interaction between the organization, the customer and supplier

(Haag et al., 2012). Businesses that are able to change their form of organization to a focus on the front line, and develop work processes connected to new technology that focus on cooperation in the global clusters of competence will be in the forefront of the global knowledge economy (Hamel, 2012; Jemielniak, 2012).

Proposition 2: Competence, service, information and decisions are moved to the front line in the knowledge organization.

Management implications: A necessary condition to achieve front line focus, is that the hierarchical and bureaucratic structures are deconstructed.

Social implications: Creativity and innovation are prerequisites for value creation in the knowledge society, and creative destruction will probably be normal.

The frontline focus helps us to understand the necessity and importance of modular flexibility (Garud et al., 2002), which we will elaborate on in the next section. A figurative presentation of the discussion in this section is shown in Fig. 3.

Fig. 3. Frontline focus

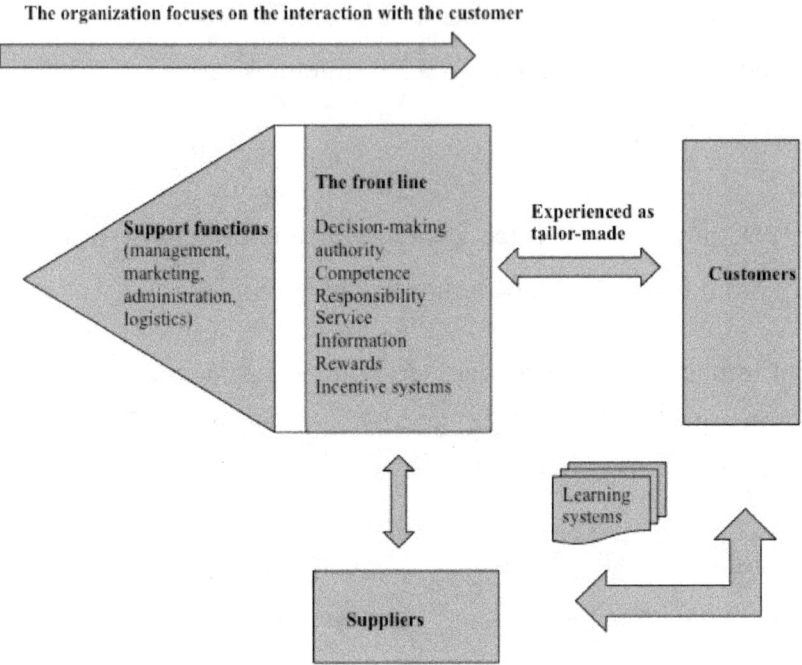

Modular flexibility

The modulization of value creation is termed here modular flexibility (Garud et al., 2002). Modular flexibility may best be understood as the globalization of production processes, and extreme specialization of work processes with a focus on core processes (Gershuny & Fisher, 2014). Of course, the economist Adam Smith as early as 1776 described a similar process when he delineated the structured activities of a pin factory. What is new in the global knowledge economy is that modular thinking is systematised on an unprecedented global scale, and that currently new technology and infostructure are used to streamline this modular logic (Brynjolfsson & McAfee, 2014).

The new organising modus is characterised by classical industrial production being re-integrated into global modules, in accordance with a logic of costs, quality, competence and innovation (Karabarbounis & Neiman, 2013). This means that parts of the production will move to areas where costs, such as for labour, are low. Other parts of the production are moved to areas where they have a specific expertise, for instance Banglore in India in the case of IT expertise. Other parts of the production are moved to areas known for design and innovation expertise (Autor et al., 2003). Metaphorically, this may be understood as a form of organization based on a "Lego principle": the individual Lego bricks are produced where they have the necessary expertise or where costs are low. Finally, the product is assembled where they have a special competence in understanding the totality of the product. Modular global manufacturing is unified and coordinated using new ICT. In other words, it may be imagined that the overall design of the product is ready (Azmat et al., 2012; Hsieh & Klenow, 2007).

Those who feel the pressure in such a structure are the industrial workers in welfare states where wages and working conditions have been negotiated over a long period of time, and are thus not competitive in relation to low-cost countries (Acemoglu, 2003: 1-37). Low-cost countries, however, can still have a highly skilled workforce and thus produce high-quality products. As mentioned, an example of this is Bangalore, India. Bangalore is the capital of the state of Karnataka. It has more than four million inhabitants and, amongst others, specializes in the education of software engineers. This example shows that it is not only unskilled and skilled labour that is ousted in the global economy, but also highly skilled knowledge workers in Western industrialized countries (Brynjolfsson & McAfee, 2014).

The logical consequence of specialization and division of labour is that it becomes progressively global, increasing competition and forcing down costs (Rios-Rull & Santaeulalia-Llopis, 2010). However, the globalization of labour and other costs leads to an increase in social conflicts (Sennett, 1998). This is, amongst other things, a consequence of established salary structures being exposed to global competition (Innerarity, 2012).

Proposition 3: Modular thinking is systematised on an unprecedented global scale

Management implication: The production system is moved in the global sphere in accordance with a logic of costs, -quality, -competence and –innovation.

Social implication: The industrial workers in welfare states will suffer.

In fig. 4 we have shown the modular logic we described in this section.

Fig. 4 Modular logic

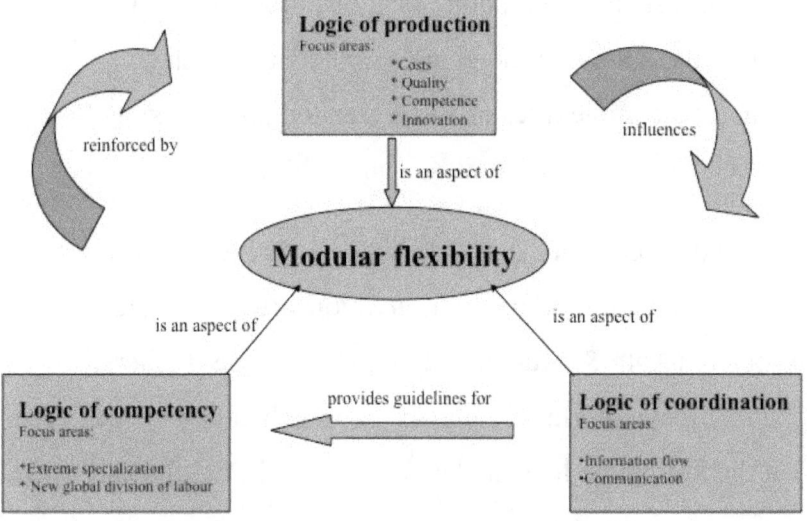

Global competence clusters

Porter (1998) argues that economic growth is largely created through local business clusters. The new technology, however, promotes a new logic of information, communication and networking in the globalized knowledge economy (Brynjolfsson & McAfee, 2014). This new logic, coupled to the fact that expertise is increasingly becoming a global resource (Autor & Murnane, 2003) available in the new infostructure, makes the global competence networks important forces in value creation (Fisher, 2006). This development promotes the idea that global clusters of competence, to a greater extent than the local clusters, are crucial for the development of innovation and economic growth (Ramaswamy & Ozcan, 2014). From such a standpoint, local business clusters may be understood in the context of the global competence clusters when explaining the complexities of value creation processes in the knowledge economy (Prahalad & Krishnan, 2008).

Structurally linked competence networks that are spread globally may constitute the most important value creation structures in the knowledge society (Auto & Murnane, 2003; Gershuny & Fisher, 2014). Global competence clusters may be geographically distributed at the individual level and consist of small, tightly-knit social networks, or be small groups with expertise; these are structurally connected through the new infostructure (Brynjolfsson & McAfee, 2014). In this way, global expertise is fully utilized for innovation and economic growth (Ramaswamy & Ozcan, 2014). In other words, the global competence clusters can be viewed together with the local clusters, and it may be imagined that the connection between the two can prove to be the main drivers of value creation in the knowledge society in the future (Acemoglu, 2003). In this context, it is the structural links that are of interest, not the local clusters or global competence networks separately.

From this viewpoint, the knowledge society and globalization mark a transition from a focus on local business clusters to a focus on links between global competence networks and local clusters with regards to value creation. This also leads to increased co-creation, interconnectedness and connectance (Ashby, 1970); these three concepts are linked to the idea that in some contexts collaboration is important, while in others competition is more crucial (Ramaswamy & Ozcan, 2014). In continuation of this trend, there is a transition from a focus on power and bureaucracy in a hierarchical system to a focus on trust and cooperation across ethnic boundaries and an emphasis on relationships in the global competence network (Sennett, 2013).

New technologies, innovation developed through global competence clusters, infostructure, modular flexibility and front line focus all serve to promote and enable the production of goods and services that can be distributed modularly in the global knowledge economy. The infostructure enables all the information that can be sent over a global network to be accessed, analysed, stored, recovered and transferred from places that can compete on cost, quality, expertise and innovation.

Co-creation is important for knowledge, knowledge transfer and knowledge integration (Ramaswamy & Ozcam, 2014; Tapscot & Williams, 2006). Co-creation involves working together to promote knowledge processes and innovation. Although competition has proven to promote productivity and economic growth, it is not necessarily this factor that should be emphasized in the global competence network. Pfeffer & Sutton (1999: 102) express this as follows: "There is a mistaken idea that because competition has apparently triumphed as an economic system, competition within organizations is a similar superior way of managing." In other words, although competition promotes productivity and economic growth in the industrial society, it is not certain that the same mechanisms apply to knowledge development and sharing in the knowledge society.

Competence development presupposes just as much cooperation in the global competence network as it does competition. The constant interaction between competition and cooperation results in co-creation becoming increasingly important for value creation. This may prove to be the fundamental driving force for value creation in the knowledge society (Ramaswamy & Ozcam, 2014). The thinking in this context is that if competition is the only prevailing principle, then everyone will protect their ideas from disclosure and knowledge development will be inhibited. If collaboration is the only principle driving the development of knowledge forward, then it seems reasonable to assume that motivation and incentives will not be optimal for the development of new knowledge. The balance between competition and cooperation, embodied in the concept of co-creation, leads to constructive criticism and the necessary scope of knowledge that exists in the network so as to promote creativity and the innovative. Instead of a zero-sum situation, a positive-sum situation will be developed where everyone wins.

Co-creation is connected to developing complementary competence teams in a global competence network. In such a social network, mentoring, cross-functional teams and collaborative teams may be developed across cultural and physical boundaries (Sennett, 2013). In addition, this presupposes a culture in which the success of colleagues is viewed as the success of the system. Shapiro & Varian (1999: 10) also emphasize the importance of focusing on cooperation in the networked economy: "…the need for collaboration, and the multitude of cooperative arrangements has never been greater than in the area of infotech". An example of the importance of co-creation is the necessity of working together to develop standards for technology and system integrations, while competing for the products and services that will be delivered using these established standards. If there is a failure to agree on standards, innovation may be hampered and value creation and economic growth may suffer as a consequence. In such a situation, the users and customers are the losers. The example concerning the development of standards shows that *cooperation is a prerequisite for competition,* in the same way as change is a prerequisite for stability. It is always a balance between competition and cooperation that creates good solutions, like the tight rope acrobat who has to find a balance between change and stability, moving his/her arms and legs in order to maintain overall stability while walking along the tight rope.

Proposition 4: Global clusters of competence, to a greater extent than the local clusters, are crucial for the development of value creation in knowledge organizations.

Management implications: There will be a transition from a focus on local business clusters to a focus on links between global competence networks and local clusters with regards to value creation.

Social implications: If global clusters of competence are essential for value creation in the knowledge society, co-creation is an important social mechanism for initiating, maintaining and strengthening these processes.

Conclusion

The chapter's research question: *What are the key value creation processes in a knowledge-based organization?*

The chapter has stressed the importance of five elements:

1. A new emphasis on the infostructure
2. A new way of organizing businesses, termed here a front line focus
3. A new way of structuring work processes, termed here modular flexibility
4. A new way of using competence, termed here global competence clusters

A focus on the frontline will promote a new kind of leader who does not have a position in the hierarchy, but has the same management functions in relation to customers as the hierarchical leader had previously. These people have high competence and are characterized by their ability to embrace simplicity.

The emphasis of the new infostructure, modular flexibility and global competence clusters requires leaders who can handle extreme complexity.

The restructuring of the world economy which follows from, amongst other things, new technologies, new structures of cooperation, global competence networks, modulization of production, and a front line focus may lead to a polarization between information-rich and information-poor systems at various system levels.

In the global economy, new geographical areas will be drawn into the economic dynamics, while other areas will be marginalized. Marginalization will result in these areas becoming economic backwaters, where value creation processes are not in tune with the global economy. Social exclusion, greater economic differences and a greater degree of individualization seem to be some of the consequences of the future global knowledge economy. For the world economy, areas that are located in the infostructure's backwater will be of little interest and not economically relevant. These areas, whether they are organizations, nations or regions, will be excluded from value creation processes. In 2013, only 39 percent of the world's population had access to the internet (Sanou, 2013). This says something both about the potential of value creation, but also about exclusion from value creation processes.

The same processes of social sanctioning, exclusion and reproduction of social inequality occur on both local and global levels. On the other hand, the flow of information pulls other areas up to economic affluence, abundance and sometimes conspicuous consumption. This polarization seems to be one of the characteristics of the knowledge society (see Castells, 1997: 70-166). Another characteristic, according to Castells (1997: 70-166), is that rich social networks are connected via mutually reinforcing value creation structures. However, we have a need for more knowledge about both value creation processes in the individual knowledge-based organizations and also in the global economy, and what the transition from infrastructure to the infostructure means to value creation on the various system levels.

Chapter 4 Prospect theory as an explanation for resistance to organizational change

Introduction

The problem under investigation is people's resistance to organizational change (Griffin & Moorhead, 2014; Harvey, 2010; Evans, 2001). This chapter investigates the following question: How can prospect theory be used to explain why people resist organizational change? The chapter aims to identify how managers can reduce resistance to change. It also aims to identify explanations of why people resist organizational change. The key concept of this investigation is how people relate to particular risks that they are experiencing.

Risk relates to our assumptions about potential outcomes and how these outcomes are evaluated by the decision-maker(s) in question (Pollatsek & Tversky, 1970, p. 541; Elster, 1986). Prospect theory was developed by Kahneman and Tversky in 1979 (Kahneman & Tversky, 1979). The theory holds that when people are faced with a risk about which they have limited information, and do not apply rigorous analytical processes, their choices will often be driven by how the information about the situation is framed either by themselves or others (Wolfe, 2008, p. 6).

The core idea of prospect theory is that people make assessments based on what they may gain or lose as the result of making a choice. One example of such a choice might be whether or not to engage actively in a change process within an organization. According to prospect theory, the possibility of losing an existing position will generate a level of resistance that will outweigh the energy and resources a person might expend in order to gain a new position (Kahneman, 2011, pp. 279-280). Most people are averse to losing something that they have already gained.

People's assessments are largely biased, distorted and not wholly reliable. Regardless of this fact, people make considerable use of these assessments in decision-making. Tversky and Kahneman found in the course of the research that led them to develop prospect theory that these assessments were heuristics or "rules of thumb" that people use in decision-making (Tversky & Kahneman, 1974, 1983). A basic assumption in prospect theory is that people use these rules of thumb without even realizing that they are doing so.

The content of this chapter is summarized in Fig. 1, which also shows how the chapter is structured. This chapter also includes a separate section that explains concrete measures that may be taken by management. These measures are based on the seven propositions developed during the course of this chapter.

Fig. 1 Prospect theory as an explanation of why people resist organizational change.

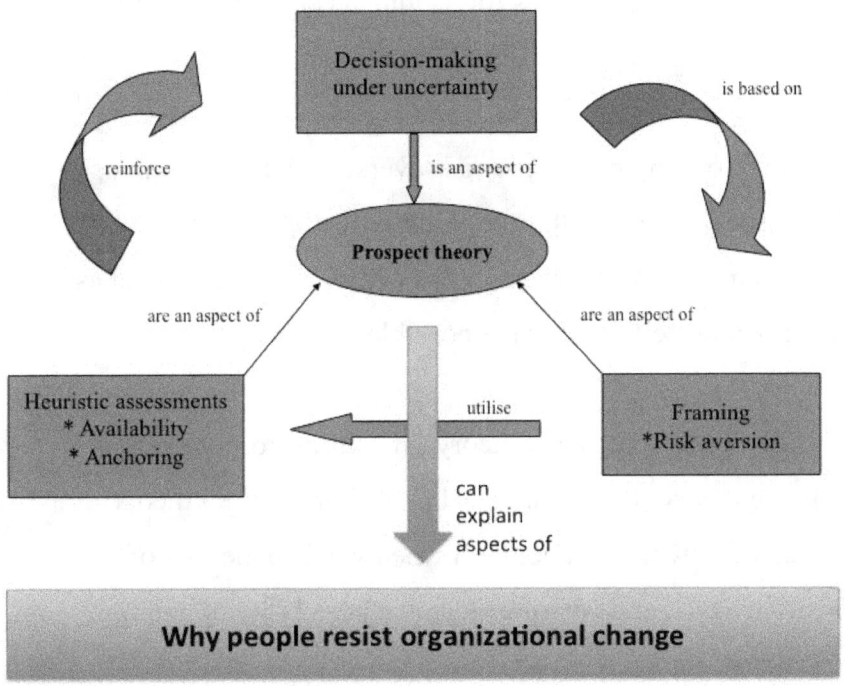

Decision-making under uncertainty

At first, it may seem reasonable to assume that people will seek out risk if they are living under poor conditions. This assumption concludes that the situation can't get worse, so people will take risks in order to improve their life situation. According to prospect theory, however, this intuitive assumption is incorrect. In fact, when a person faces the possibility of losing the rights, power, positions, income, etc., that he or she has already achieved, they will seek to retain what they have achieved and are reluctant to change (Kahneman & Tversky, 2000, p. 22). People avoid participating in change processes for as long as possible because they risk losing what they have achieved.

The explanation of why people are risk-averse is linked to what is known in prospect theory as the "certainty effect" (Kahneman & Tversky, 2000, p. 17). Very broadly, this effect can be described as a preference for the certain over the possible.

What is different about prospect theory, in contrast to, for example, rational choice theory (Kahneman, 2011), is that prospect theory takes account of how we will act both when we face the loss of rights, positions, etc., and when we face the possibility of gaining the same kinds of rights, positions, etc.

If one is in a situation where one risks losing positions one has gained, one will be willing to take a risk in order to retain one's current position. If one faces a situation where one has an expectation of gain, then the probability is great (paradoxically) that one will prefer to secure what one has already achieved.

Prospect theory uses the phrase "reference point" to denote the point at which we take action in the various situations described above. Our assessment of a situation is determined by the position we are in when we undertake the process of assessing the situation. The key psychological concept of prospect theory is that people dislike the idea of losing a position but like the idea of winning one (Kahneman, 2011, p. 281). The important point here, however, is that people will commit more effort to preventing a loss than achieving a potential gain (Kahneman & Tversky, 2000, p. 22). In addition, Kahneman and Tversky state that people's commitment increases when they are trying to prevent a loss but decreases when they are trying to gain something (Kahneman & Tversky, 2000, p. 17). For all practical purposes, this means that the energy and resources a person will use to prevent a loss will increase in proportion to the likely size of the loss. The converse is not true in respect of a gain.

Proposition 1. If management structures their change project to take account of the fact that people will resist change because they risk losing what they have already achieved, then the change project will have a greater chance of success.

Practical implications. People will expend more energy and resources on preventing losses than on gaining new positions.

Management implications. Management should be aware that if employees face a situation that offers a potential benefit then the likelihood is great that they will prefer instead to secure their existing positions.

The "reflection effect" reverses the "certainty effect". As a rule of thumb, resistance to change is reversed when the possible gains are between 1.5 and 2.5 times greater than the status quo (Kahneman, 2011, p. 284). It is when gains reach this point that participation in organizational changes comes into consideration. This concerns when one can choose between retaining that which is established and secure on the one hand, and investing resources in a process of change on the other. The choice will, in the context of the "reflection effect", be related to the expectation of future opportunities to choose to participate in change, rather than to retaining a reliable and proven solution.

A third psychological effect that prospect theory refers to is the "isolation effect" (Kahneman & Tversky, 2000, p. 17). This refers to people's tendency to discard elements that all choice situations have in common, leading to inconsistent preferences. The focus in this context is on what separates the choice options, i.e. that which creates a distinction (Tversky, 1972). Among other things, this effect means that choice options are broken down and framed in terms of a probability of loss or possibility of gain. If a change situation is presented as involving a probable loss, then one will maintain the status quo. However, if the change is presented as an opportunity to make very large gains, say more than 100 per cent of what one already has, then it will be possible to apply the certainty effect and the reflection effect to move someone from a status quo situation to a situation involving investment and commitment to a change project. Presenting information in this way means that people are willing to change, even if they do not have complete information about the outcome.

Fig. 2 shows a model of how the three effects (certainty effect, reflection effect and isolation effect) can vary in relation to each other, explaining resistance to change during organizational changes.

Fig. 2: Resistance to change in organizations.

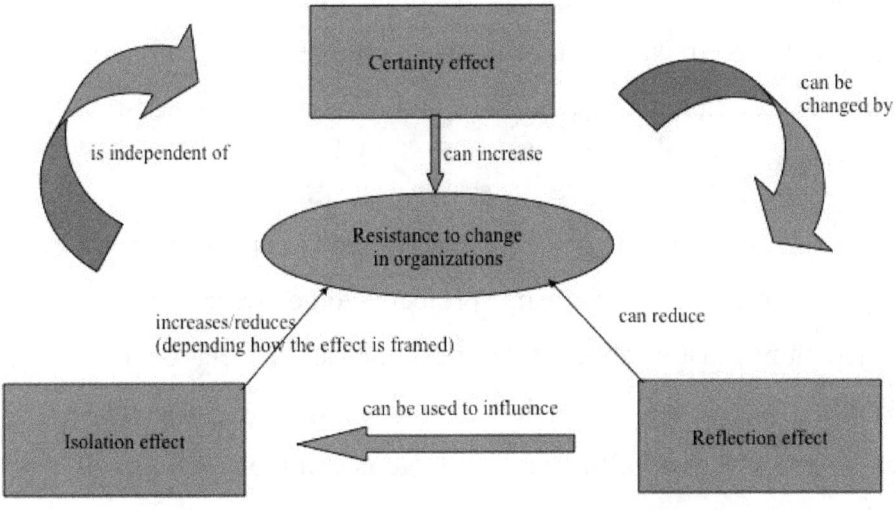

In prospect theory, psychological assessments are related to three elements: losing, winning and the reference point (McDermott, 2001). The reference point is, as a rule, related to expectations or the status quo (Kahneman, 2011, p. 282). What is perceived by some as a large gain may be perceived by others as insignificant (Vis, 2010).

In prospect theory, there is always a reference point related to expectations about a possible gain. This is the basis for assessing whether to seek to secure what you already have or to seek any changes that present themselves.

The practical choices are often complex and involve a risk of loss and a possibility of gain. Consequently, we operate, in effect, with a subjective assessment of expected usefulness in relation to our choices. There are risks and uncertainties associated with choices: the choices are often not that clear-cut and frequently include mixed assessments.

A useful rule of thumb for managers that can encourage people to engage in an organizational change project is to be aware that the expected gains must be about 100 per cent or more in relation to the status quo. The tendency will then be to choose the option for potential gains in spite of the fact that there is still the possibility of loss (Vis, 2010). Experiments have shown that the rate of loss aversion increases with increasing investment, so the more that is at stake, the greater the possibility of gain must also be if one is to choose to fully embark on a change project (McDermott, 2001). However, the loss aversion rate does not increase proportionally with the possibility of loss. For instance, in situations where life is threatened or people are exposed to bankruptcy, the degree of loss aversion is dramatically high. There are certain actions that are unacceptable no matter what the possible final gain (Kahneman, 2011, p. 284). This may explain why some people enter into organizational change processes while others don't. In practice, the degree of loss aversion can be much greater for some people depending on their life experiences (Vis, 2010). For instance, individuals and groups accustomed to experiencing losses, such as professional gamblers, military officers, financial brokers, vulnerable and marginalized groups, etc., may have a greater tolerance of losses.

Proposition 2. If management presents the changes as an opportunity to achieve a gain of more than 100 per cent of what employees already have (the status quo), then it is highly probable that employees will consider the change project as positive.

Practical implications. If management wants to reduce resistance to change, then they should present the possible gain as being more than 100 per cent.

Management implications. Management can reduce resistance to change in organizations by taking advantage of the interaction between the certainty effect, the reflection effect, and the isolation effect.

Framing

Prospect theory assumes that people do not act on the basis of full information when making decisions. They instead usually act on the basis of available information. Following from this, the theory does *not* assume that people are fully rational when making choices. The theory investigates how people act in practice when making choices, asking, for example, how they use intuition when making choices in uncertain situations. When faced with a choice between an uncertain change that may offer future opportunities and a current status quo situation, people often act on the basis of the proverb "A bird in the hand is worth two in the bush". In other words, we tend to choose the safe option over the one which is uncertain but which offers opportunities.

Some people also tend to be optimistic about any given situation they find themselves in. Such a bias is both a blessing and a risk, says Kahneman (Kahneman, 2011, p. 255). The so-called "pessimists" and "optimists" have been examined and discussed in several empirical studies (Seligman, 2006; Snowdon, 2001; Fox, Ridgewell, & Ashwin, 2009). The optimists, Kahneman writes, are "…the inventors, the entrepreneurs. …They got to where they are by seeking challenges and taking risks" (Kahneman, 2011, p. 256).

Although most of us are risk-averse, some of us are optimists and willing to participate in change processes even though expectations do not offer 100 per cent or greater gains regarding the possible outcome.

Proposition 3. If management discovers who the optimists are and assigns them to the change project, then the probability is great that the change project will succeed.

Practical implications. We tend to opt for that which is established and safe and discard the opportunity for potential gains. This conservative element in human decision-making may also partly explain why there is a time lag between an assumed necessary change and the impact of change in the organization.

Management implications. It is easier to involve the optimists in a change project than the pessimists. Management should therefore search for optimists and let them be the agents of change for the project.

It is the framing aspect of prospect theory that has received most attention (Wolfe, 2008, p. 9). Framing can be understood as the way in which "individuals and groups make sense of their external environment" (Boettcher, 2004, p. 331). We use framing to organize and understand the world around us. Using information frames, we are able to perceive a phenomenon, issue, event, etc., in a new way. Prospect theory argues that framing is used to make choices and assumptions in relation to future outcomes (Tversky & Kahneman, 1981). How information concerning our choices is presented is an important consideration in the framing phase of prospect theory (McDermott, 2001, p. 21). We can also frame that which is rational so that it appears reasonable, even though something that is rationally justified might not necessarily have a reasonable justification. Sense and rationality can be contradictory terms, although they may also be congruent.

The most general part of framing in prospect theory concerns how a loss is framed in relation to a gain. This may be achieved by selecting information frames that result in the loss or gain appearing in a different light to an individual.

Losses and gains are considered in relation to the status quo and what will serve one's own interests or those of the system (Mandel, 2001). The framing or editing of a given situation may be termed prospect theory's initial phase (McDermott, 2001, p. 20). In many situations we are not aware of what opportunities exist or the possible outcomes of our choices. Consequently, we often construct possible alternatives and the results of pursuing them before making a decision; this is the creative aspect in any decision-making process. It is during this stage that management should think through the importance of which information frames they will use. In other words, according to prospect theory we adopt a kind of bias. We have an aversion to losing what we have already gained; therefore, our choices will be influenced by how the choices and the prospective results of these choices are framed. How the information framework is used is consequently not an insignificant part of the outcome of how people react to change projects in organizations.

Tversky and Kahneman express this clearly by saying that "…choice depends on the status quo, or reference level: changes of reference point lead to reversals of preference" (Tversky & Kahneman, 2000, p. 143). In our context, this can explain the importance of how information frameworks are presented in relation to the extent of resistance to change in organizations.

One of the principal assumptions of prospect theory that emphasizes the importance of information frames is that "losses and disadvantages have greater impact on preferences than gains and advantages" (Tversky & Kahneman, 2000, p. 143). Loss aversion in prospect theory has major implications for how people in organizations relate to change and how their preferences change when reference points shift over time. Information frames are concerned with moving the reference point, not providing valid information that is completely reliable.

Proposition 4. If management frames information concerning the change project as representing a large gain for everyone, then the probability is great that employees will consider the change project in a positive light.

Practical implications. The assumption here is that it is people's perception of the reference point that will move them in one direction or the other.

Management implications. Management should be cautious about introducing too many changes simultaneously and carrying out rapid changes in succession because this may easily lead to erratic behavior in organizations. This can lead to a loss of efficiency and increased resistance to change projects in the organization.

Heuristic assessments

There are four basic heuristic assessments that Tversky and Kahneman have described (Beach & Connolly, 2005, pp. 81-83; Kahneman, 2011; Tversky & Kahneman, 1974, 1983). These are:
     1. Representativeness and randomness,
     2. Anchoring
     3. Availability
     4. Validity.

In this chapter, only anchoring and availability will be discussed because these are the most relevant in explaining why people oppose change in organizations.

Anchoring. A boat at anchor can move around, but the anchorage will always be its pivot point. To move the anchor point, you have to take up the anchor and physically move it to another place. If you have first dropped anchor, then you have also chosen the pivot point or the point around which negotiations will revolve. The anchor effect does not concern a lack of or incorrect information; it is an effect that seems to apply even if we have sufficient information (Chapman & Johnson, 2002).

When we are trying to estimate something, such as the probable success of a change project, the development of property prices (Northcraft & Neale, 1987), the benefits of adopting a new idea in an organizational change project, etc., we will often begin by making an initial estimate. This is our so-called "anchor". We will then make adjustments in relation to the anchor (Beach & Connolly, 2005, pp. 82-83). However, if the anchor is not placed correctly, then the probability is great that the final results will also differ from what was originally planned. This calls to mind a popular quotation from Ibsen's *Peer Gynt*: "But when the starting point is weakest the result is often the most original".

Thus, according to prospect theory, where you set the anchor in relation to a prospect will affect subsequent behavior (Kahneman, 2011, p. 119). Whether one chooses to invest in a change project is also related to the anchor of how project information is framed, i.e. the risk in relation to winning or losing what has already been gained. If you take the risk of investing in a change project, how much is the potential upside? We have seen above that the potential upside should be more than 100 per cent. However, experiments have also shown that the gain should range between as much as 150 and 250 per cent if one is to take the risk of investing in something new. It is the anchor related to risk aversion that is interesting from a change perspective, because it says something about how willing the individual is to engage in a change project.

An interesting aspect from an information perspective is that people consider their potential gains and losses from the anchor that has been set even when it has been set randomly (Chapman & Johnson, 2002:120-138). It appears that the anchor effect operates in such a way that the end result on average does not vary by more than 55 per cent from the anchor that was originally set. In experiments, this seems to apply even if the anchor is not taken into account (Kahneman, 2011:124). From an information perspective, this is important knowledge for management or those who are selling a change project.

An interesting point related to anchors is that they affect us, although we are aware of this (Wilson & Brekke, 1994:117-142). Anchors are used to extract and select information, integrate this information and then formulate a response to another party (Chapman & Johnson, 2002, p. 126). This says something about the strength of the anchor effect.

Proposition 5. If management uses the anchor effect to control people's resistance to change, then the probability is great that employees will engage positively in the change project.

Practical implications. The anchor effect explains aspects of why people oppose changes in organizations and may be used to reduce people's resistance to change.

Management implications. Management should be aware of the fact that the anchor effect may differ by 55 per cent from a set anchor.

Availability.

If information is available at regular intervals, then it is easy to refer to such information (Beach & Connolly, 2005, p. 82). We say in such situations that the information is available in one's memory. However, it is not only information that is often repeated that is available for retrieval in one's memory; events that have left a deep impression also have the same availability effect. For instance, emotional childhood experiences, air disasters, genocide, pestilence, economic crises, change projects that went wrong resulting in mass dismissals, etc., are easier to recall from memory than, for example, the fact that thousands of people are killed every year in traffic accidents.

It is therefore understandable that journalists, historians, and others compare the 2008 economic crisis with the 1930s depression because examples from the 1930s depression can easily be retrieved from memory. However, it is dangerous to make such a comparison if the 1930s depression can only to a small extent be relevantly compared to the 2008 economic crisis. If politicians initiate measures for the recent economic crisis on the basis of knowledge of initiatives that should have been adopted in the 1930s, this may create more problems than it solves. This example says something about the importance of information availability.

The question "Why do we believe more in one type of information than in another type?" may, among other things, be answered by the fact that some types of information are easier to retrieve from memory than others. In other words, the information we believe in is more "true" than other types of information. In this context, the expression "availability cascades" used by Kuran and Sunstein (Kuran & Sunstein, 1999) is of interest. By this they mean that we are to a certain extent controlled by the image of reality that is constructed by the media because it is easier to retrieve from memory.

How easily information may be retrieved from memory when faced with a situation demonstrates the availability proposition's relevance. The availability proposition can be expressed in the following way: the more easily information enters into our consciousness, the greater the likelihood that we will have confidence in that information. In other words, we believe more in the type of information that is available in the memory than information that is not so readily available.

What is important to note concerning the availability proposition is that information does not necessarily need to be credible as long as it is available. It is, inter alia, in such contexts that Kahneman asks us to use System 2 (Kahneman, 2011), which he uses to refer to analytical thinking to check the validity of information. However, it is the availability proposition that prevails, because most people are not trained in statistics and analysis of information.

Proposition 6. If management uses the information available in the memory of employees and develops an anchor in relation to this information, then the probability is great that employees will consider the change project in a positive light.

Practical implications. We have a tendency to distort information and believe that the information that is easier to retrieve from memory is more credible than information that emerges after thorough analysis.

Management implications. Management should use information about change projects that can easily be compared with historical or contemporary events that employees can easily identify with.

A variation of the availability proposition is the affect proposition, which concerns how emotionally affected you are by the situation that is being assessed. In other words, the perceived risk of a project may be reduced if you are more emotionally affected by the project. In the real world, "we often face painful trade-offs between benefits and costs" (Kahneman, 2011, p. 140). Whether you choose to engage in a change project or prefer the status quo may depend on how emotionally affected you are by the project.

Proposition 7. If management succeeds in getting employees emotionally involved in the change process, then the probability is great that they will consider the perceived risk associated with such changes as small.

Practical implications. Whether people are willing to engage in a change project or try to preserve the status quo may depend on the extent to which they experience changes as emotionally attractive.

Management implications. To increase the emotional reward of a change, it seems reasonable to assume that management should use the anchor effect and framing.

Specific measures that management can implement

On the basis of the seven propositions described above, the following measures may be considered to reduce resistance to change in organizations.

Decision-making under uncertainty

Risk aversion. As a general rule, people seek to retain what they have already gained and are reluctant to change. We often operate on the basis of intuitive rules and psychological principles that govern the framing of information about our choices. However, these rules and principles are not necessarily rational or logical.

Management can apply this knowledge in order to reduce resistance to change by:

1. Crisis understanding: point out the necessity of the changes.
2. Psychological safety: point out that the proposed changes do not carry any risk of loss for employees.
3. Expectation management: point out the benefits of the changes.

The potential must be more than 100 per cent. There are three effects that may be employed in efforts to reduce resistance to change in organizations. The first is called the "certainty effect". This implies that one chooses what is certain, i.e. what you already have, rather than that which is probable and offers opportunities, such as engaging in an organizational change project where the outcome is uncertain. The second effect is called the "reflection effect", which reverses the "certainty effect" if there are expectations of future gains of more than 100 per cent stemming from the change. The third effect is called the "isolation effect", which refers to a tendency to discard elements that all choices have in common and to focus on what separates the choices (Kahneman & Tversky, 2000, p. 17).

Management may increase the likelihood that employees will engage with and dedicate themselves to a change project by presenting the changes in such a way that they will lead to improvements in the proposition to employees that accrue to gains of more than 100 per cent across a number of change proposal elements.

Framing

We seek safety. We have a tendency to be conservative in our thinking: we wish to retain that which we have and are reluctant to adopt that which is new. One way for management to engage with this conservative aspect of our thinking may be to engage those who have little risk aversion in relation to the change project as project managers at various levels. The rationale for this strategy is provided by Kahneman. The people who are responsible for the implementation of a change project are often more optimistic than those who are not in this position, and optimists are more positive about change than pessimists. Kahneman underlines this supposition with the following statement: "…the people who have the greatest influence on the lives of others are likely to be optimistic and overconfident, and to take more risks than they realize" (Kahneman, 2011, p. 256).

Management should identify the optimists in the organization because they will most likely participate in the change project even though the possible future gain is not more than 100 per cent. They should also identify the sceptics to the change project and give them responsibility for some of the changes.

Erratic behavior. If management introduces too many consecutive changes this can easily result in the organization becoming unsettled. Consequently, employees may become reluctant to accept more changes. This may result in alienating those who initially supported the need for change and give more weight to those who are opposed to change.

Management may prevent such erratic behavior by involving employees at an early stage in the planning of changes. In the planning phase they should frame information so that the change project is presented as a win-win solution, where employees make large gains and risk losing little. In this way everyone is informed about what must be done, why it should be done, how it should be done, and the desired effects of the changes.

Heuristic assessments

Anchoring.

Use of the anchor effect for strategic purposes can result in us making choices we would not normally make. Countless experiments have shown that people's choices correspond to the anchor they use, even though the anchor may be irrelevant, random and evidently incorrectly set (Epley & Gilovich, 2002, p. 139). If you have a strong expectation of future success, then this expectation, this anchor, influences your behavior in the present (Switzer & Sniezek, 1991). Taking into account the anchor effect can help reduce resistance to change in organizations (Tversky & Kahneman, 1974). Moreover, it is advantageous to frame your project with a possible future gain of 150–250 per cent in relation to the status quo. An important point concerning the anchor effect is that it controls our behavior, even though we have sufficient information about the situation. Management can use this insight by setting the anchor in such a way that expectations are motivating for the individual.

Availability.

The availability proposition developed by Tversky and Kahneman in 1972–1973 (Kahneman, 2011, p. 129) can be expressed in the following simplified form: the easier information is to retrieve from memory, the greater the cognitive authority that information has. If you want to sell a change project, then it can be advantageous to link it to a media event that has a positive connotation.

Management can reduce resistance to change by linking the change project to a media event that has a strong positive connotation (cascade effect).

Emotional strength. One relies more on information that reinforces our perception of the object, event or action if we are emotionally attracted to the object. When this happens we will take greater risks, and we will have a tendency to assign less importance to information that is critical and rely more on information that is positively charged in relation to the change project.

Management should encourage employees to become emotionally connected to the change project because this will trigger individual commitment and dedication to change.

Conclusion

In this chapter we have attempted to answer the following question: how can we use prospect theory to explain why people resist organizational change? To answer this question seven propositions have been developed.

There are three magnitudes around which the propositions are organized. These are: decision-making under uncertainty, framing, and heuristic assessments (anchoring and availability).

In Decision-making under uncertainty there are two propositions. Proposition one is related to the knowledge that if people risk losing what they have already achieved, they will resist change. Proposition two says that the probability is high that employees will consider the change project as positive, if they think they achieve a gain of more than 100 per cent of what one already has (the status quo).

In Framing there are also two propositions. The first proposition in framing tells management to discovers who the optimists are, and assigns them to the change project. If they do so, then the probability is great that the change project will succeed. The second proposition in framing says that management ought to frame information concerning the change project as representing a large gain for everyone. If they do so, then the probability is great that employees will consider the change project in a positive light.

In Heuristic assessments there are three propositions in two categories: anchoring and availability. We have one proposition in Anchoring. This propositions states that if management uses the anchor effect to control people's resistance to change, then the probability is great that employees will engage positively with the change project.

We have two propositions in availability. The first proposition states that if management uses the information available in the memory of employees, and develops an anchor in relation to this information, then the probability is great that employees will consider the change project in a positive light.

The second proposition in availability tells that if management succeeds in getting employees emotionally involved in the change process, then the probability is great that they will consider the perceived risk associated with such changes as small.

Taken together the seven proposition have been compiled into a system, defined here as a "mini-theory", about how resistance to organizational change can be reduced. For each of the seven propositions we have discussed practical and management implications.

Chapter 5 Knowledge management and knowledge worker performance

Introduction

Possibly the most important contributions to progress in the 20th century were made by technological developments in general and information technology in particular (Baird and Henderson, 2001). In the 21st century, according to Drucker (1999a: 135), the focus will be on knowledge workers, particularly on ways of motivating them and increasing their productivity.

While the most important contributors to productivity in the industrial society were industrial workers, whether skilled or unskilled, there is much to suggest that the most important contributors to productivity in the knowledge society will be knowledge workers, whether highly or extremely highly educated (May et al., 2002).

A literature review conducted by Wong (2013) in connection with his PhD thesis concluded that there have been relatively few studies worldwide of knowledge workers' productivity. Wong found no major studies that had conducted an empirical investigation of this topic.

Several researchers have highlighted the importance of – and the difficulties associated with – managing these new knowledge workers (Mabey et al., 2002; Smith et al., 2005; Alvesson, 2000; Swart, 2007; Guest, 2011). According to Hlupic (2014), a significant problem in knowledge organizations today is that management paradigms and management practices have not kept up with the times. Senior managers who follow outdated management practices will structure and manage their organizations using a hierarchical approach based on command and control principles (Hlupic, 2014).

The aim of this chapter is to develop a mini-theory concerning the management of knowledge workers and ways of increasing their productivity. In this context, we use the term "theory" to refer to a system of propositions (Bunge, 1977; 1985). Our mini-theory may also be understood as an example of an HPWS (high performance work system) (Takeuchi et al., 2009:1069; Messersmith et al., 2011: 1105).

A system of HR practices that promotes knowledge workers' productivity may also be understood as research relating to HPWSs (high performance work systems) (Godard, 2001; 2004; 2010; Godard and Delaney, 2000). Takeuchi et al. (2009:1069) define this as: "a group of separate but interconnected human resource practices designed to enhance employees' skills and performance." Analogously to this definition, in this chapter, we define an HPWS for knowledge workers as: *A system of HR practices at individual and organizational level that promotes knowledge workers' productivity.* The concept of a "system" in this definition takes account of the description "separate but interconnected", used by Takeuchi et al. (2009:1069).

Traditionally, HR practices have focused on the individual (micro) level, particularly on areas such as recruitment, selection, remuneration, information-sharing and skills development (Huselid, 1995; Takeuchi et al., 2009). Having reviewed research relevant to HPWS, Messersmith et al. (2011:1105) emphasize that researchers do not have a clear understanding of the relationship between HPWS and organizational performance. This chapter attempts to make a small theoretical contribution as to how this relationship may be assumed to exist. We do this by formulating six propositions that are intended to explain some of the social mechanisms likely to affect knowledge workers' performance.

A good deal of research has clarified that HPWSs function by enhancing skills development, motivation and worker participation (Liao et al., 2009; Lepak et al., 2006; Wegge et al., 2010). None of these researchers has focused, however, on knowledge businesses and the productivity of knowledge workers. We take as our starting point Drucker's (1999; 1999a) six assumptions concerning factors likely to promote the productivity of knowledge workers (Maciariello, 2014; Maciariello and Linkletter, 2011).

The problem for discussion is as follows: How can managers promote the productivity of knowledge workers?

Our objective in this conceptual study is to develop a system of propositions, i.e., a theory (Bunge, 1977; 1985) regarding factors likely to promote knowledge workers' productivity.

The chapter may contribute to research and HR practices in three areas. First, each of the HR practices we propose for promoting knowledge workers' productivity may be taken as a starting point for HR practices. Our conceptual model may be used as a basis for implementation (Fig. 1). Second, each of the propositions we suggest for developing operational hypotheses may form a starting point for future research. These hypotheses may then be subjected to empirical testing. Third, the operational hypotheses that are generated from these propositions may be subjected to empirical testing in order to identify the variances in and strengths of each proposition in relation to its effect on knowledge workers' productivity.

In general, a knowledge worker's capital is his/her competence and what he/she does with that competence (Scarbrough, 1999). Davenport (2005) says that these workers "think for a living." As noted by Pyröriä (2005), there is no completely unambiguous definition of a knowledge worker. What we do know is that high-performance systems will influence a knowledge worker's attitudes and behaviour. We do not know, however, what factors will promote the productivity of an individual knowledge worker (Kehoe and Wright, 2013; Drucker, 1999).

The OECD has described a knowledge worker as *a person whose primary task is to generate and apply knowledge* rather than to provide services or produce physical products (OECD, 2000a; b; c; d; e; 2001). This may be understood as a formal definition of a knowledge worker. This definition does not restrict knowledge workers to creative fields, as is the case with, for example, Mosco and McKercher (2007: vii–xxiv). The OECD definition also allows for the fact that a knowledge worker may perform routine tasks. The definition also does not limit the type of work performed by knowledge workers on tasks relating to creative problem-solving strategies, unlike the definition provided by Reinhardt et al. (2011).

Historical context

The first researcher to address the concept of the knowledge worker and the importance of this category of worker was Drucker (1959; 1999; 1999a). Drucker's precise area of focus was the productivity of this new type of employee.

As early as 1967, however, Galbraith assumed that a new class of technical specialist would emerge and take over much of the work (Galbraith, 1967). Fritz Machlup suggested as early as 1958 that one-third of the workforce in the United States was responsible for performing information-related tasks (Machlup, 1962; 1981; Machlup and Kronwinkler, 1975).

The OECD has shown that in 1970, 40 per cent of the workforce in the United States and Canada performed work relating to information processes (Pyöriä, 2005:118). Today, 75-80 per cent of employees in North America are estimated to have jobs that in one way or another cause them to be categorized as knowledge workers (Ramirez and Nembhard, 2004; Haag et al., 2012). These new workers are relatively highly paid, have a high status and are mainly university-educated (Reich, 1991).

Assumptions concerning knowledge workers

Knowledge workers use a great deal of time searching for information – some empirical studies suggest as much as 38 per cent (McDermott, 2005). They are also to a large degree separated from their leaders in the sense that it is their output that is controlled, not their work processes (Cortada, 1998; Hannah et al. 2015; Drucker, 1999). Empirical studies indicate that these workers quickly become burned out and that they are managed through normative expectations (Jemielniak, 2012).

The new knowledge workers may be involved in various projects in various intersecting networks, which may partly compete with each other. Knowledge workers in such businesses and networks increasingly function as "free agents" in relation to these intersecting interests. The free agents manage their own careers and income flow, says Hedberg (1997). They create their own jobs in or outside of a larger business or network. Projects these free agents create are connected to competence, ambitions and a desire to create their own lifestyles (Autor et al., 2003; Brynjolfsson and McAfee, 2014). These independent agents are included in projects and networks with more or less independent contracts to one or more systems.

Drucker's drivers for increasing knowledge worker productivity are: focus on primary tasks, results orientation, innovation orientation, recognition of knowledge-sharing, self-management and continuous development of skills (Drucker, 1999; 1999a). We will focus on these elements in this chapter.

Tapscott and Williams (2006) indicate the link between knowledge workers and innovation. Tapscott and Williams also note that global competence and the Internet are important prerequisites for developing innovation in the global knowledge economy.

Important motivating elements for the new knowledge workers are independence, self-actualization, co-worker influence, self-management and a focus on symbolic distinctions rather than bureaucratic positioning or attainment of power through traditional hierarchies (Wegge et al., 2010: 154-171). They are motivated by themes, problems, phenomena, challenges and co-worker influence (Innerarity, 2012; Davenport, 2005; Drucker, 1986; 1999; 1999a; Tapscott and Williams, 2006).

They have little or no loyalty or identity with the organization that happens to pay their wages (Jemielniak, 2012). Their identity is not the organization to which they are currently linked but rather the problem and theme areas, such as the development of new software (Autor et al., 2003). The "good life" seems to function as a fundamental basis for knowledge workers, although what constitutes the "good life" is not unambiguous and common to them all (Reinhardt et al., 2011). However, they seem to have in common that income (in one form or another) is important, so that they have the freedom to develop their own definitions of the "good life" (Davenport, 2005 Drucker, 1999a). One could say that knowledge workers do not work to live; their jobs *are* both their lives and their hobbies. Therefore, the "good life" is connected to the way of working, not a strategy towards the "good life" in retirement. Consequently, it is a focus on the primary task that the knowledge worker is interested in and that motivates him/her (Drucker, 1999; 1999a; Jemielniak, 2012). Therefore, profit orientation or focus on output is also an important control factor for knowledge workers. They need to know what, when and how much they are expected to deliver. Beyond this output, it will not be expedient to control working hours, work processes or inputs in production, because this may easily be counter productive (Davenport, 2005; Drucker, 1999a; Jemielniak, 2012).

Conceptual model

We have developed a conceptual model (Fig. 1) that captures the essential features of what we have discussed in the introduction and that answers the question: How can we promote knowledge workers' productivity? Fig. 1 also shows how the chapter is organized.

Fig. 1. The productivity of knowledge workers: A conceptual model

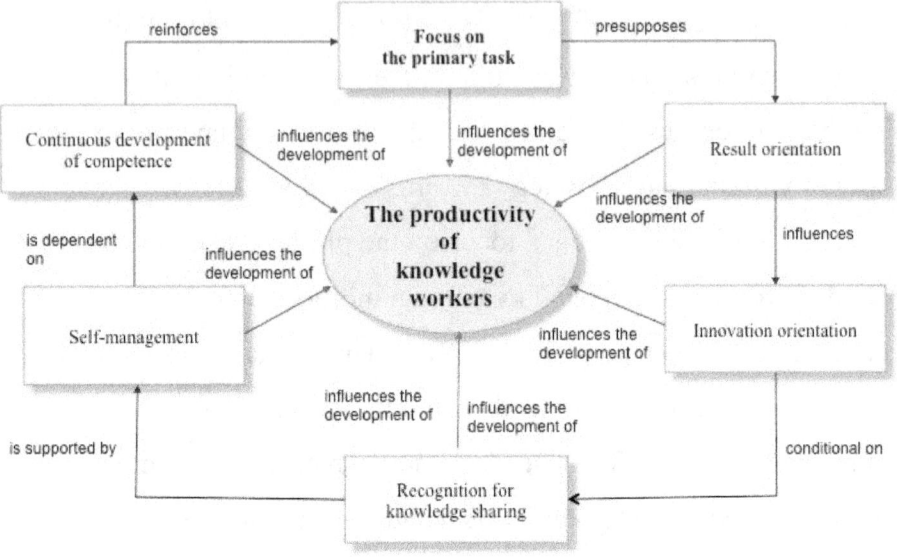

Organization

First we will sequentially look at each element in Fig. 1 and explain each one in relation to its theoretical basis. Then, we will also develop practical tools for use by management and the HR department for the employment of these HR practices at the organizational level. Finally, we will design a proposition for each element. The system of propositions will constitute a mini-theory (Bunge, 1977; 1985) for knowledge worker productivity. The mini-theory is shown in its entirety in the conclusion in response to the chapter's problem for discussion. The six practical tools developed for management and the HR department may function as a starting point for HR practices at the organizational level, related to knowledge worker productivity.

Focus on the primary task

Explanation

What is the primary task? This is the key question related to knowledge worker productivity (Drucker, 1999a: 144). Stafford Beer (1995) says that the primary task is what the system is designed to do. In the case of an agricultural worker, industrial worker or employee in the service sector, it is relatively easy to answer the question. However, for knowledge workers, the answer is somewhat more complex. This is, inter alia, on the grounds that we cannot quite define how a knowledge worker performs his/her work, even though we know what the primary task is (Davenport, 2005).

In the case of knowledge workers, we have not yet reached the stage where we ask what their primary tasks are (Drucker, 1999a: 144). It seems clear that most knowledge workers spend a good deal of their time on tasks that are not their primary tasks (Autor et al., 2003). For instance, an engineer, a nurse and others are often called away from their primary tasks to attend a meeting, fill out a report, document their work, conduct inspections, etc. (Wong,

2013). In most cases, these tasks prevent knowledge workers from doing their primary tasks, and these non-primary tasks could be performed by other employees at a much lower cost than when using specialists. For instance, a survey of nurses showed that they doubled their productivity[4] by transferring tasks that were not defined as their primary tasks to others (Drucker, 1999a: 145-146).

When it is apparent what the primary task is, then one can advantageously use a method from "lean thinking", involving the elimination of non-value-added activities (NVA) (Liker, 2004; Womack, 2003). Eliminating non-value-added activities may be used to reduce costs and increase the productivity of knowledge workers. Non-value-added activities are all the activities and processes that do not create value for the customer. In this context, the customer concept of lean thinking ("the person next in line") is important (Womack, 2003; Liker, 2004). The primary task should be structured, i.e., all the activities and processes that do not specifically relate to the primary task should, as far as possible, be reduced and preferably eliminated or transferred to others. For instance, some of the activities that are considered necessary but are not part of the knowledge worker's primary task can be taken over by others. When specialists in the fields of medicine, nursing, engineering or other fields use substantial resources to perform work not requiring their professional skills, this indicates that there

---

[4] The primary task in this case was defined as "patient care". Productivity was measured in the number of hours they used for patient care.

is great potential for productivity improvements.

Practical tools for the HR department: Focus on what we are supposed to do

Crucial questions that the HR department should clarify relating to the individual knowledge worker (Drucker, 1999a: 145):

1. What is/are your primary task(s)?
2. Which tasks do you perform now? In other words, is there a gap between what your primary task is and what you actually do?
3. What prevents you from performing your primary task?
4. How can these obstacles be removed?

In relation to these questions, and referring to a study of nurses' primary tasks in a major hospital, Drucker says the following: "asking the questions and taking action on the answers usually doubles or triples knowledge worker productivity, and quite fast" (Drucker, 1999a: 145).

Proposition 1: The greater the extent to which knowledge workers are focused on their primary tasks, the more likely it is that their productivity will rise.

Result orientation

Explanation

A principal function of management is to provide feedback on employee behaviour and performance in relation to reaching the goals of the individual and the organization (Beer, 1995; Boselie et al., 2005). However, according to Latham et al. (2007: 365-381), it is important that the following process steps are followed so individual and team performance can be promoted:

- First, the result that individual or team is expected to deliver should be clarified.
- Second, the development toward the result must in some way be remunerated, so that the individual, team and management know they are on the right track, i.e., a feedback analysis must be carried out.
- Third, management should continuously provide responses to the feedback analysis.
- Fourth, management should evaluate the results and make the necessary decisions based on the evaluation.

In result orientation, the first step is essential, because it is here that the knowledge worker, together with the management, defines what the individual or the team of which he/she is a member is expected to deliver. Performance will involve both quantitative and qualitative goals. If no such targets can be defined, it will be difficult for management to provide meaningful feedback. The objectives will, as a rule, be many, and therefore, the evaluation instrument should be able to handle sufficient variety to capture all the targets toward which the individual and team are working. The objectives must also be designed so that if the knowledge worker or team performs more than expected, this will affect the assessment and the reward system positively (Wagner and Goffin, 1997). If this does not happen, then it is highly probable that the individual or team settles on the expected level (Cardy and Keefe, 1994).

Practical tools for the HR department: What can I contribute that makes a difference?

The following questions will be important for the HR department to clarify, relating to the individual knowledge worker (Drucker, 1999a: 180):

1. What should I contribute?

It is not what the individual necessarily wants to do or what the manager says he/she should contribute that is inherent in this question. It is the assumption that the individual knowledge worker should contribute that little extra to the organization in those areas where he/she has expert knowledge. This will not necessarily coincide with what a leader believes he/she should be able to do. For instance, by using the example of a symphony orchestra, this idea becomes apparent. A symphony orchestra may be a collective of musicians, but the performance of the collective is dependent upon the skills of each specialist within the orchestra; in other words, they perform as a collective, but they have developed their specialties alone.

When the above question has been answered, it may be appropriate to ask three continuation-questions (Drucker, 1999a: 181): Is this what I want? Is this what I do best? Is what I should contribute something I am most motivated to do?

However, Drucker emphasizes that merely doing what one wants to do can lead to disaster, whereas what one should do more often leads to success, a conclusion he reached after considering many historical examples where this was the case (Drucker, 1999a: 181-182). In other words, the idea inherent in the question above is to focus on one's own resources and not to divide them into what you want to do or what you are told to do.

2. Where can I make a difference?

It is the difference where you should contribute that really makes a difference. It is in those areas where you can make a difference, where you should develop your expertise. In other words, you should extend yourself beyond your comfort zone to make a difference for others, not necessarily for yourself. In seeking to make a difference for others, you are pro-socially motivated (Grant and Berg, 2010). The pro-socially-motivated employee cares about and helps other colleagues. He/she is concerned that what he/she does will have importance for others.

The supplementary questions to question two are the following (Drucker, 1999a: 183):
What does the situation demand? How can I contribute to making a difference in the specific situation? What results must be achieved for me to make a difference? The achievement of results are the key point in question two, not that one does what one wants to do.

Proposition 2: The greater the extent to which knowledge workers are focused on the results they are to deliver, the more likely it is that their productivity will rise.

Innovation orientation

Explanation

Innovation is here understood as any idea, practice or material element that is perceived as new for the person using it (Zaltman et al., 1973). There are three points that are important in this definition (Johannessen et al., 2001).
- How does the individual perceive the innovation?
- The degree of novelty that determines whether it is an incremental or radical innovation.
- The requirement that the market must adopt an idea before it can be called an innovation.

Ideas are seen as the smallest unit in the innovation process (Hamel, 2002; 2012). However, this refers to the ideas that are in the process of development and not fully developed ideas. Before an idea can be characterized as innovative, it must prove to be beneficial to somebody, i.e., the market must accept the idea and apply it. Consequently, the creative process of innovation is here understood as the benefit it has for a market (Amabile, 1990;

Johannessen et al., 2001: 25). Thus, it is not sufficient that an idea is new for it to be considered an innovation. An idea may have a great degree of novelty, but if it is of no benefit to anybody in the market, then it has no innovative value.

Innovation orientation presupposes: "a clear road map for making innovation everyone's job" (Hamel, 2008: xix). To achieve this, it is essential that businesses develop an information structure (infostructure) for creativity, so everyone can participate, not just the chosen few. This idea is an extension of Hamel's law of innovation (2002; 2007). The "law" states that only between one to two of one thousand ideas become innovations in a market. Therefore, an infostructure must be created to ensure that ideas are continuously produced in a business.

Practical tools for the HR department: How to design an organization's idea-development processes.

It will be important for HR departments to clarify the following points when promoting idea-development in an organization. Just as product development has its own logic, then idea creation for innovation also has its own logic. Idea-development processes may be divided into four parts:
1. Involve as many as possible (Von Hippel, 2005).
2. The number of ideas is crucial (Hamel, 2007; 2008).

3. Allow the possibility of adopting ideas from outside the organization (Chesbrough, 2003; 2006; Chesbrough et al., 2008).
4. Select ideas with the potential for value creation (Skarzynski and Gibson, 2008).

Proposition 3: The greater the extent to which knowledge workers focus on developing ideas to foster innovation, the more likely it is that productivity will rise.

Recognition for knowledge-sharing

Explanation

There are few individuals, if any, that can develop knowledge on their own. An important point regarding organizations and institutions is that we depend on each other to develop knowledge. Therefore, every company should develop a system for transfer of experience and knowledge-sharing. Thus, we can become effective with the help of others. To achieve this, an organization needs to develop a system for organized and continuous improvement processes, or what the Japanese call "kaizen" (Maurer, 2012). This may be done in many ways. One way is to systematize lessons learned through information-sharing and organizational learning systems. Information is the knowledge worker's key resource

(Drucker, 1999a: 123). Consequently, leaders should ensure that information is available, because it is information that enables knowledge workers to do their work effectively.

Recognition for sharing information and knowledge is primarily based on what others need to be effective, i.e., the focus is not on oneself. One should take responsibility for others and start a process in the organization, where one will also ultimately benefit from such a knowledge-sharing culture. By taking this perspective, a culture of knowledge-sharing can be created, which affects the entire communication climate in the organization (Bratianu, 2015). The management's responsibility in such a context is to support information and knowledge-sharing. The argument here is that if such knowledge-sharing does not exist in the organization, then everybody will lose by it (Leistner, 2010). This is of course not a new insight; Barnard pointed this out as early as 1938 in his book *The Functions of the Executive* (Barnard, 1974), and later Mintzberg also pointed it out in 1973 in his book *The Nature of Managerial Work* (Mintzberg, 1997).

Skarzynski and Gibson describe one way of organizing transfer of experience (2008: 45-85). First, teams of four are formed, comprising employees from different departments within the organization. The members represent a cross-section of employees, both in terms of expertise and experience. As a starting point, these teams should be dedicated to the tasks at hand, which is to develop, acquire and test new ideas. Each group is autonomous in relation to the organizational hierarchy (line) and the functional areas from which they originate and is accountable only to the manager in the organization, who is responsible for the process. Each group then takes a specific perspective in the process. Four perspectives are distributed among the four groups (Trompenaars, 2007):

1. Challenging prevailing thinking in the organization or industry.
2. Discovering underlying trends.
3. Examining your organization as a system of competences.
4. Understanding the unarticulated needs of the customers[5] or potential customers.

The focus of each of the groups is new opportunities for value creation based on new ideas or the linking together of old ideas. The opportunities that are selected are organized as projects, and then pilot projects are developed and tested in the market.

The organization of a pipeline for the transfer of experience is a strategic responsibility (Harris, 2005: 34). The aim is to transform the organization into a learning social system that integrates the knowledge that is spread throughout the organization (implicit knowledge), while it simultaneously utilizes the tacit knowledge of the organization (Pfeffer and Sutton, 1999) and accesses the

---

[5] Customers, users, patients, students, i.e., all the groups who are directly affected by what the system is supposed to deliver.

knowledge that people don't know they have (hidden knowledge). Kirzner (1982) says that hidden knowledge is possibly the most important knowledge domain for creativity, innovation and entrepreneurship. By integrating the explicit knowledge, tacit knowledge, hidden knowledge and implicit knowledge of the organization with the external knowledge base, it is possible to develop a culture of experience-sharing (Seirafi, 2015).

Practical tools for the HR-department: Information analysis

It will be important for the HR-department to clarify the following questions concerning the individual knowledge worker:
1. What information do I have that others need so they can do their job effectively?
2. What information do I need in order to do my job effectively?
3. Where do I find this information?
4. Who else in the organization can benefit from this information?
5. When do they need this information?

Proposition 4: The greater the extent to which knowledge workers receive recognition for sharing their knowledge, the more likely it is that productivity will rise among all knowledge workers in an organization.

Self-management and self-organization

Explanation

In the emerging knowledge economy, knowledge workers must to an ever-greater extent create their own careers. They must increasingly learn how to lead and organize their own work (Drucker, 2005). In this context, Drucker says: "They will have to place themselves where they can make the greatest contribution" (1999a: 163). Important in this context is the fact that not only the surroundings will change and affect businesses, but knowledge workers will also change, which in turn will also affect the businesses where they work. The biggest change for knowledge workers is that they must learn to manage themselves (Stacey, 1996). They must learn to recognize their own strengths and weaknesses; and they must know where they can make a difference. They must plan, develop and use a strong and robust network. They must plan for their next job, because they are very likely to work longer and outlive the organization they are working for (Stanford, 2013; Drucker, 1999a: 163-165).

It is through knowing their own strengths and weaknesses,

opportunities and obstacles that individuals can develop their personal change skills and achievements, so they can compare themselves with the best; they can also develop their personal motivation strategies, effectiveness skills and reputations (Roberts et al., 2005).

Whoever is able to manage themselves will be the winners in the knowledge economy, says Drucker (2005: 100). Most people know their weaknesses to some extent, but to a lesser extent their strengths (Drucker, 2005: 100). Gaining greater insight into one's strengths can develop performance (Roberts et al., 2005). In very few cases, if at all, is it possible to develop talent on the basis of weaknesses. Consequently, the individual must know specifically what he/she is does well and then reinforce this position.

It is only when the options' window is great and the options many, as is the case in the global knowledge economy, that there is really a need to develop insight into what one does well and then develop these aspects.

Before, when stability of the external world was relatively great and the pace of change relatively small, the need for continuous development of individual strengths was less important than in today's global knowledge economy, where the pace of change is rapid and complexity great (Stiglitz and Greenwald, 2015).

It is the emergence of the global knowledge economy that makes self-management and self-organization an important challenge for the individual knowledge worker. Self-management is based on interaction skills and emotional intelligence (Goleman, 1996). This means that every aspect of feedback is central to self-management. One aspect of feedback that is not immediately evident is the feedback type termed "feed-forward" (Hansen, 2015). Feed-forward is regarded here as an expectation mechanism. It seems reasonable to assume that our expectations influence our behaviour in the present. It is therefore important that we make explicit to ourselves the expectations we have of a situation. By making expectations explicit, we have a greater opportunity to learn from our experiences and thus improve our performance. Feedback is the most important element in interactive skills and emotional intelligence (Goleman, 1996; 2007). In this way, there is a close connection between interactive skills, emotional intelligence and self-management. Analysis of feedback is a sure way to identify our strengths and then reinforce these (Wang et al., 2003).

It is the constant interaction between feedback analysis and the development of strengths (that we are not fully aware of) that makes self-management an important part of the individual's personal development in the knowledge society.

Self-management involves the transition from the question – What should I do? – to the question – What should my contribution be?

(see Drucker, 2005: 106). The latter question is related to making a difference that really matters for one's self and others. To do this, the individuals must develop aspects of themselves (that perhaps they are not even aware of) to utilize the potential to make a difference. In this context, the individual must gain self-knowledge and also actively take relationship responsibility to become familiar with the strengths of others. In this way, it will be possible together to develop a difference that really matters, which is the first step towards a qualitative idea, which has the potential to be an innovation (Bateson, 1972: 271-273).

The underlying elements of self-management, as we have emphasized them above, are the following:

- Feedback analysis.
- To understand others' goals and challenges and be able to take the others' perspectives (mentalizing).
- To focus on what you do well.
- To be part of a network that is committed to developing the reciprocal strength of what you and they already do well.
- To develop a personal story.

Practical tools for the HR-department: Strengths analysis

The following questions will be important for the HR-department to clarify relating to the individual knowledge worker:

1. What are my strengths?
2. How can I make a difference that will really be a difference and help create the creative new idea? Bateson (1972: 271-272) expresses this as follows: "the difference that makes a difference or an idea."
3. How do you carry out feedback analysis? When making a decision, you write down your expectations about the results. After a period of time, say, six to twelve months, you examine how the real results were compared to those expectations you had written down. Afterwards, you analyse why there was a gap between your expectations and the results. When this feedback analysis is performed over two or three years, the probability is high that you will have uncovered a pattern in your behaviour and become aware of your strengths (Drucker, 1999a: 164-166).
4. Drucker emphasizes that it is just as important to remedy your bad habits as to be aware of your strengths (1999a: 167). This is, says Drucker, things you do or do not do that negatively affect performance. Feedback analysis will clarify how bad habits and attitudes inhibit performance. This may be the inability to follow through on a project that is well planned and initiated. You should be aware that it is not faith or ideas that moves mountains but bulldozers, says Drucker (1999a: 167). In our context, this means that implementation capacity is essential, if a project is to be completed by set goals and standards.

Proposition 5: The greater the extent to which knowledge workers can exercise self-management, the more likely it is that productivity will rise.

Continuous development of skills

Explanation

A special feature of the knowledge society is that information flows freely, at a rate that does not incur time lag, and where financial, technical and cultural decisions are global (Castells, 1997). Florida (2008) has positioned the tension between the global and local levels to a few key urban areas in the world. The global level has acquired a geographic basis, focused on a few mega-cities, where key decisions are made that will have consequences for most people, instantly or with a time lag. This leads to, among other things, the fact that the knowledge society to a greater extent than the industrial society is characterized by a rapid rate of change, a lack of stability and high complexity. One of the consequences of the increasing complexity is that "crises hit unexpectedly and as a matter of routine" (Webster, 2002: 133). Another of the consequences is that those businesses that fail to adapt quickly will be rapidly swept away by the global economic juggernaut. Those who survive will be those who are mobile, who can build relationships quickly, create networks and participate in knowledge production (Baird and Henderson, 2001). Global competence networks are a natural consequence of the developments we have suggested above, where the mobility of capital, labour and services are underlying elements (Urry, 2004). Urry (2004: 190) says that this mobility concerns "peoples, objects, images, information and wastes." Mobility is closely related to the transitory. The mobile and the transitory may be understood as a tripartite structure. At the bottom exist the local and regional clusters that produce matter-energy and information for the global market. The clusters are relatively close in geographical terms and, therefore, termed by Porter (1998) as business clusters. There exist relatively clear boundaries around these clusters. In the middle of the structure, one can imagine the global networks of competence (Hamel, 2012) that have contact with the various local and regional clusters. The global competence networks connect the local and regional clusters in the global space. On the third level, patterns emerge that change character and direction like liquid (see Bauman, 2011). These are the virtual global competence clusters.

The local and regional business clusters are visible, while what constitute mobility are the global competence networks and the patterns that crystallize in these (Ulrich, 2013). Metaphorically, this may be understood as a transition from solid to liquid form in the social structures. The stability of the liquid structures is the pattern that connects the global networks of competence, what we refer to here as the virtual global competence clusters. The virtual global competence clusters may be divided into political, social, economic, technological and cultural patterns. It is when these five patterns interact that one may perceive the overall pattern. In the global knowledge economy, it seems reasonable to assume that those who control this pattern set the conditions for economic development.

Knowledge and skills transfers occur at both the local and regional cluster levels, as well as within and between the global competence networks (Sassen, 2002). In the innovation literature, the focus has for a long time been on the national and regional innovation systems and innovation in single businesses (Skarzynski and Gibson, 2008). If the assumption of mobility as a core phenomenon in the global knowledge economy is correct (Urry, 2004), then it seems reasonable that the focus will turn more toward global competence networks.

HR practices at the macro level can include organizational design (Ulrich, 2013), globalization implications (Brynjolfsson and McAfee, 2014; Garud et al., 2002), also called international HR (Boselie, 2014: 5), as well as work with the emerging global competence clusters (Autor et al., 2003; Chang, 2008). Such global competence clusters may be found in the IT sector, for instance, in Bangalore, India, which employs hundreds of thousands of engineers in the software sector (Gershuny and Fisher, 2014; Hannah et al., 2015). These global competence clusters will most likely have an impact on HR departments in, for example, Norwegian companies competing for this type of expertise in the Norwegian market.

OECD (2001) also emphasizes global competence networks as crucial for economic growth, although they use the term innovative clusters. The purpose of innovative clusters and global competence networks is the development, dissemination and use of new ideas that promote wealth creation. According to OECD (2001), the overarching drivers of innovation in individual businesses are: globalization, the knowledge-based economy, ICT and stability in public institutions. There is much to suggest that a greater degree of integration and cooperation between private and public sectors at the national and regional levels is an important prerequisite for initiating the innovative locomotive effect. The global competence networks are metaphorically the energy source that sustains the motion of this locomotive. It would be counterproductive to replace the locomotive once in motion. Conversely, the individual carriages of the locomotive (read: organizational level) may be changed, depending on their competitive position. The individual passengers on the train create ideas and knowledge through the processes that may be called creative chaos. In this way, we will arrive at a tripartite of the prerequisites for global competence networks. At the individual level, creative chaos occurs. At the organizational level, there will be creative destruction. At the social and global levels, creative collaboration takes place. These three processes create innovation and economic growth as an emergent, not as a "future perfectum", a planned process with given results. An emergent occurs if something new pops up on one level that has not previously existed on the level below. By emergent, we mean: *"Let S be a system with composition A, i.e., the various components in addition to the way they are composed. If P is a property of S, P is emergent with regard to A, if and only if no components in A possess P; otherwise P is to be regarded as a resulting property with regards to A"* (Bunge, 1977:97).

A prerequisite for the reasoning above is that tension and competition at one level require collaboration at another level. Competition and cooperation are both necessary if one is to develop innovation and economic growth in the same manner that stability and change are necessary for flexibility. Too much of one (stability) leads to rigidity, and too much of the other (change) leads to chaos. Understood in this way, emergents cannot be planned. The point here is that knowledge workers must continually develop their competence, so they are receptive towards the creative and new that emerges as a result of emergents.

Practical tools for the HR-department: Skills and competence analysis

The following questions will be important for the HR department to clarify, related to the individual knowledge worker:

1. Skills and competence analysis consists of four elements:
    a. First, clarify your strengths.
    b. Then, identify the habits that limit performance.
    c. Most important of all, suggests Drucker (1999a: 167), are your behaviour, attitudes and how to relate to others. Competence is only a necessary prerequisite for success; it is not a sufficient one. How you act and present yourself are possibly the most important factors. The rationale is that these factors say something about whether you can manage to get others on-board, or if you are left alone with a project. Drucker (1999a: 167) speaks figuratively of lubricating relationships to avoid frictions, conflicts and tensions.
    d. The next part of the skills and competence analysis, which Drucker (1999a: 168) recommends, is that you do not spend time trying to improve areas where your competence is low. You should focus on and reinforce the areas where you already have a relatively high level of competence in the first

place. There are too many organizations, says Drucker (1999a: 168), that try to improve people's expertise where they do not have any particular advantage in the first place. This only results in the organization developing many employees to a mediocre level of competence.

e. Knowing how to learn is crucial when mastering skills. Do you learn best by listening or reading? To clarify this may increase your ability to learn radically. Do you learn best by working in a team or by working alone? Do you learn best by taking notes or by summarizing what you have heard or read? When you ask people about how they learn best, it is surprising how many have insight regarding how they learn. However, it seems there are few who use this insight to develop their competence on a daily basis (Drucker, 1999a: 173). Drucker's point is that only those who act on the basis of an understanding of how they learn best perform the best. How you perform is closely linked to how you learn. Therefore, it is important to relate how you best learn to how you act on the basis of this insight.

Proposition 6: The greater the extent to which knowledge

workers have opportunities to continually develop their skills, the more likely it is that their productivity will rise.

Conclusion

In this chapter, we have investigated the following problem: How can managers promote knowledge workers' productivity? The short answer to the problem can be summarized in the mini-theory developed in this chapter. The mini-theory consists of six propositions:

Proposition 1: The greater the extent to which knowledge workers are focused on their primary tasks, the more likely it is that their productivity will rise.

Proposition 2: The greater the extent to which knowledge workers are focused on the results they are to deliver, the more likely it is that their productivity will rise.

Proposition 3: The greater the extent to which knowledge workers are focused on developing ideas to foster innovation, the more likely it is that their productivity will rise.

Proposition 4: The greater the extent to which knowledge workers receive recognition for sharing their knowledge, the more likely it is that productivity will rise among all knowledge workers in an organization.

Proposition 5: The greater the extent to which knowledge

workers can exercise self-management, the more likely it is that their productivity will rise.

Proposition 6: The greater the extent to which knowledge workers have opportunities to continually develop their skills, the more likely it is that their productivity will rise.

Theoretical implications

We have discussed the point made by Wegge et al. (2010) that in all probability, the greatest motivating factor for knowledge workers is the influence of co-workers, both operationally and strategically. The proposition that follows from the chapter by Wegge et al. may be formulated as follows: *The greater the extent to which knowledge workers are influenced by their co-employees, the more likely it is that their productivity will rise.* The only reason that we have not included this proposition in our mini-theory is that we have attempted to model this chapter in accordance with Drucker's ideas.

Practical implications

These six practical tools for HR departments may form the starting point for developing a "tool chest" for HR managers that may be used to promote knowledge workers' productivity. With this tool chest, HR departments will gain a resource that they can use to promote knowledge workers' productivity. The tools in this chest will sometimes relate to HR practices at an individual level, while at other times, they will relate to HR practices at an organizational level. To be specific, tool no. 3, listed below, will relate to HR practices at an organizational level, while the other five tools will relate to HR practices at an individual level.

The HR manager's tool chest for promoting knowledge workers' productivity is shown in its entirety below.

1. *Focus on what we are intended to be doing.*
2. *What can I contribute that will make a difference?*
3. *How does the organization go about designing idea development?*
4. *Information analysis.*
5. *Strength analysis.*
6. *Analysis of skills and competence.*

Further research

Further research into knowledge workers' productivity may be conducted along three different lines of enquiry. First, one might attempt to investigate the individual propositions by means of a longitudinal case study. Thereafter, it would be advantageous to apply the knowledge gained from the longitudinal case study to develop – on the basis of the propositions – hypotheses capable of being put into operation, and then to test these hypotheses by means of a larger empirical study.

Along with the six propositions in the mini-theory developed in this chapter, the seventh proposition regarding co-worker influence should also be included, both in the longitudinal case study and the larger empirical study.

Chapter 6 Strategic HRM: A theory for the ambidextrous organization –a new function for HR departments

Introduction

Traditionally, organizational structures have focused only to a limited extent on the co-existence of operational management (exploiting "the now") and innovation (exploring "the new") (Maier, 2015). Although projects have certainly been initiated with this idea in mind, this work has been little institutionalized and has generally been too constrained by existing structures. This was noted by Tushman & O'Reilley as early as 1996. The concept of an ambidextrous organization was first applied by Duncan (1976). It is March (1991), however, who has been credited with developing the concepts of exploring the future and exploiting the present, which correspond with what is meant by ambidextrous organization. The unique characteristic of an ambidextrous organization is its ability to adapt to changes in external conditions while at the same time generating its own future by means of, among other things, improved performance, growth and innovation. Ackoff (1981) developed a method whereby organizations could simultaneously adapt to current conditions and create their own futures. In this chapter, we use the term "strategic HRM" to refer to the choices that an organization makes in relation to organizing work and using its workforce (Boxall & Purcell, 2011:65).

The concept of the ambidextrous organization can be understood in at least three ways. The first perspective is linked to the development of two structures, one focused on exploiting the present and the other on exploring the new (Adler, et al., 1999; Tushman & O'Reilly, 1996; Nadler & Tushman, 1997). The second perspective is known as "contextual ambidexterity". This perspective applies behavioural and social methodologies in an effort to integrate, at an organizational level, the exploration of the new and the exploitation of existing resources (Gibson & Birkinshaw, 2004; McCarthy & Gordon, 2011). A third perspective is an increasing focus on the role of management at both team and organizational level in ensuring organizational ambidexterity (Jansen, et al., 2009; Cao, et al., 2010; Rosing, et al., 2011). This third perspective was also highlighted in 2004 by O'Reilly & Tushman as one of the major challenges for management.

After studying how 85 companies structured their innovation efforts, O'Reilly & Tushman (2004) found that an ambidextrous structure resulted in the best performance within existing operations and was the most successful in promoting innovation. An ambidextrous structure means an organization is able to manage daily operations on the one hand, but also that opportunities to research new ideas are encouraged and given autonomy on the other.

Of the 85 businesses examined in the research project, some opted for a functional design, with project teams integrated into existing organizational structures. Others employed cross-functional teams, with team members operating within the established organizational structure but outside the existing management hierarchy. Yet others formed "unsupported teams" that operated outside existing organizational and management hierarchies. A final group opted for an ambidextrous structure, with project teams that were autonomous yet still operated within the framework of the company as a whole. All of these teams had their own processes, structures and cultures.

The findings of O'Reilly & Tushman (2004) were overwhelming. Regarding the launching of radical innovations, they found that none of the cross-functional or unsupported teams and only a quarter of the teams with functional designs were able to produce radical innovations. However, among the ambidextrous organizations, 90% were successful in producing radical innovations. Empirical research has shown that this type of organizational design is best for producing both incremental and radical innovations (O'Reilly & Tushman, 2004; Thora & Munir, 2011).

An ambidextrous organizational structure has also been found to have other benefits in addition to producing successful innovation. Organizations with an ambidextrous structure show an improved rate of growth (He & Wong, 2004). A study of 41 businesses (Gibson & Birkinshaw, 2004) and a similar study of 34 high technology businesses showed a higher rate of growth in businesses with ambidextrous structures (Chandrasekaren et al., 2012). There are many examples of businesses where an ambidextrous structure has resulted in success, for example Apple, General Radio, Nordstrom, and British Airways (Tushman & O'Reilly, 1996).

It is important to emphasize, however, that an ambidextrous structure is not favourable in all circumstances. As a rule, one can say that in situations where there is rapid change, significant turbulence, and very dynamic and complex external circumstances, an ambidextrous structure will be preferable (Jansen, et al., 2006). In other cases, the advantages of an ambidextrous structure are more debatable (Raisch & Hotz, 2010).

Interest in ambidextrous organizational design has been growing ever since the publication of chapters by Duncan (1976), Tushman & O'Reilly (1976), and March (1991), and especially since the publication of O'Reilly & Tushman's chapter of 2004 (Reinmoell & Reinmoeller, 2015; Maier, 2015; De Wit & Meyer, 2014).

As O'Reilley & Tushman (2004) wrote, the metaphor for

ambidextrous organizational design is the Roman god Janus. Janus looks backwards and forwards at the same time. This is how we have chosen to approach the task of evolving a theory for ambidextrous organizational design. We look back at Beer's theory, which dates from the 1980s, and use this as the basis for designing an ambidextrous organization. Like the god Janus, we choose also to look forwards by suggesting that HR departments may play a decisive and innovative role in the future of work, according to this theory.

In this chapter, we propose a perspective based on integration, whereby we describe, analyse and discuss a theory that incorporates both structural and contextual ambidexterity, and focuses on the role of management in promoting ambidextrous organizational designs.

Some authors suggest that young, creative businesses are the most likely to succeed both in generating their own radical innovations and in tackling the arrival of new radical innovations on the market (Schneider & Veugelers, 2010). Adopting an ambidextrous structure may also be a way for larger and older businesses to achieve their own radical innovations, while at the same time tackling the arrival of radical innovations on the market and coping with daily operational requirements (De Wit & Meyer, 2014:211-216; Reinmoell & Reinmoeller, 2015; Maier, 2015).

As in other areas of life, we may have something to learn from nature when designing ambidextrous business structures (von Krogh et al., 2012). Businesses are still mainly structured according to the "heat, beat and treat" theories prevalent in the industrial era. These may however be less appropriate for a knowledge society (Baird & Henderson, 2001). In order to develop ambidextrous organizations, we must look to theories based on analogies to the human brain and body (Beer, 1979; 1981; 1995).

In the chapter, we take as our starting point a "forgotten" theory from the 1980s (Beer, 1979; 1981; 1995). We give this theory new life by suggesting that parts of it may show us precisely how to design ambidextrous business structures, while at the same time suggesting a possible new innovative function for HR departments in this type of ambidextrous organization. In this way, we will both give this "forgotten" theory new life and identify an important new aspect of the role of HR in the future.

Stafford Beer devoted much of his life to answering the following question: *What would an organization look like that could survive in a world that is characterized largely by change, turbulence and complexity?* (Beer, 1995) Beer took as his starting point one of the most complex systems in existence: the human brain. Transferring this approach to organizational design, Beer determined that systems organized like the human brain consist of five different sub-systems, together with an extremely powerful connection to the external world. This implies that he viewed organizations as open systems (Whitehurst, 2015).

The following discussion briefly presents the five different sub-systems and the entire system as Stafford Beer envisaged them. The discussion will also outline methods for the systems' use by organizations that could succeed in simultaneously achieving effective everyday operations, while also supporting a separate function that addressed the future and the need to innovate.[6] Later in the chapter, we will explore each of the five sub-systems in greater depth.

Brief description of Beer's theory

System one represents the operational level in an organization. System one accesses resources from the outside world to ensure the system's survival. The organization gains access to these resources, such as money, information, expertise, raw materials etc., by delivering to the outside world that which it is willing to pay for, i.e. value creation for the customer, user, patient, student,

---

[6] For pedagogical reasons, we have decided here to focus on a single level of recursion. Beer worked with several levels of recursion, with the whole point being that each System one unit shall contain within it the design of the whole. This can be understood as a kind of holographic organization where the whole is represented in the parts. As already mentioned, for pedagogical reasons we will not include different levels of recursion in the following presentation. Readers interested in learning more about recursion are advised to refer to Beer (1995).

and so on. System one thus constitutes the organization's core processes. What these core processes are will become apparent by answering the question: What is the organization designed to do? In other words, what is the organization's purpose? The system's purpose then forms the basis of the core processes that it is designed to carry out. For instance, in the case of a university these core processes as a rule will consist of teaching, research and dissemination activities.

The challenge for most systems is that they usually have several core processes and sub-processes in system one. It is therefore important to have a system (functional area) which coordinates the various processes in order to avoid tension, conflict and chaos. Beer terms this system two. In the case of a university, this will involve an appropriate balance between teaching, research and dissemination. Within the area of teaching, schedules and resource allocation will function as a coordinating mechanism that prevents conflict and chaos. At an airport, traffic controllers will also have a similar role. In a local community, the police may have a coordinating function. Within system two, we find norms and values, procedures, rules, budgets and accounts which all facilitate the coordination of the various core processes in system one. Another feature of system two is to monitor the output of system one. This is accomplished by establishing upper and lower control limits. If these thresholds are exceeded then information concerning the variance will be sent to system three, which then intervenes directly in system one (ref. Fig. 2).

System three concerns "here-and-now" management. This feature is often described as the middle management function in an organization. System three receives information concerning variances from system two, and makes the necessary corrections on the basis of this information. This is done through management, control, resource allocation, communication, etc. The time dimension in system three is primarily short term, and the focus is on the daily running of the organization. However, it is important for the system's survival that someone is also responsible for monitoring possible future developments. This function is performed by system four, which we will call here keeping "an eye on the future". This monitors both the known and unknown future in the short and long term, although the main focus is on more long-term thinking through an emphasis on future possibilities. The most important key words are adaptation, change and innovation. System four can employ future-oriented research methods, such as scenario planning, scenario learning, trend analysis, early warning systems (internal and external), incident analysis, Delphi method, etc.

System five is responsible for top-level management that ensures the necessary direction and balance within the whole organization; in private and public companies, this will typically be the responsibility of the Board. The focus within system three will be on efficiency, productivity and profitability, while system four will be concerned with creativity, change and innovation. There will almost invariably be tensions between the firefighting of system three in its short-term crisis mode and the more long-term thinking that system four handles, says Beer (1995). Consequently, system five is concerned with ensuring a proper balance between system three and system four.

Based on this explanation we have developed the following problem for discussion:

Problem for discussion: How can we design organizations to resolve the paradox of the co-existence of operational management (exploitation) and innovation (exploration)?

In order to find an answer to the problem we have chosen two questions for research:

Research question: In light of Beer's theory, what new functions relating to innovation may exist for HR departments?

Fig. 1 shows a representation of that which is described in the introduction; it also shows how the rest of the chapter is organised.

Fig. 1 Beer's theory of ambidextrous organization

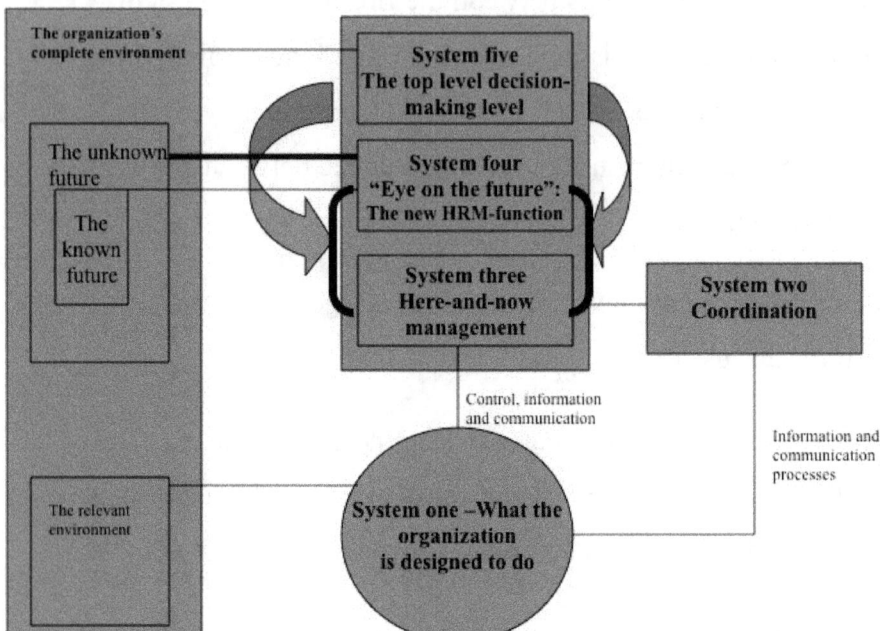

What are the new functions of HR departments?

In this section, we will attempt to answer the research question by explaining, analysing, and discussing system four. The links between systems one, two, three and four, with system five as a balancing system between systems three and four corresponds to the theory concerning ambidextrous organizations (O'Reilly & Tushman; 2004; 2007; 2011). As mentioned above, system one is autonomous and largely self-organizing, while system three has a management and control function via system two. System four, however, is not placed on the central command axis, but delivers ideas and feasibility analyses to both system three and system five.

The new HR-function: "An eye on the future"

System four ensures that the whole organization can change when it is needed, i.e. when changes in the environment are such that the organization would benefit from change. To accomplish this task it is important that system four has an overview of all activities and processes taking place throughout the whole system, as well as the processes in the outside world that are of importance to the organization. In other words, system four must be able to theorize the activities of the organization and its environment; in this context Rios and Schwaniger refer to "the Conant Ashby Theorem" (Rios, 2012:12; Schwaniger, 2008:20-22).

In addition, System four should carry out the following tasks for the whole organization:

1. It should create an explicit theory of the value creation processes that occur in the organization.
2. It should theorize the organization's environment, so that the organization as a whole at any time is aware of the opportunities and threats that exist.

3. It should address the organization's future, both the expected and the unexpected.
4. It should identify and monitor what is happening internally in the organization.
5. It should provide information and knowledge about different possible futures for the organization so that the organization can rapidly act if trends in the outside world may come to threaten the organization in the future.
6. It should provide knowledge about the possible choice of action if any of the scenarios occur.

In this way system four, and the HR function become a potential for flexibility that is designed into the organization.

System four sends the necessary information about the outside world and what happens internally in the system, both to system five and to system three. In this way, system four provides the appropriate information to the decision-makers, so that they are able to make the necessary decisions (Beer, 1995 115).

According to Stafford Beer, system four must also bear in mind the four principles of organization (Beer, 1995: 29; 43; 47; 55). These principles may be described as follows:

1. Management strategies should be designed so that they aim to achieve external and internal adaptation so that stability is maintained. This paradox that stability requires change is an important point; this is no more difficult to understand

than the fact that a tightrope walker maintains equilibrium by constantly shifting position.
2. The information channels that are used to collect information and make decisions must have the necessary capacity to avoid "information input overload" (Miller 1978: 123).
3. There should be as little as possible, and ideally no lag between information and decision-making. Management must in this regard also focus on the feedback system and threshold values in the system.
4. Decisions should be based on reliable and real information.

How should system four prepare for an organization's future? Stafford Beer talks about two possible futures for any system (Beer, 1995: 119). On the one hand, there is the "known" future, i.e. the future you can predict with a relatively high degree of probability. For instance, relatively reliable data may be obtained concerning the so-called "known" future, such as: the increase in population growth; the need for housing construction; the elderly as an increasingly important market segment; how wage developments in the developing world will affect the economy in developed countries; etc. This may be done using various future scenario methods.

However, such methods cannot be used to say anything about the so-called unknown future. In this case, other methods should be used, such as, scenario techniques, the Delphi method, "foresight" and similar tools. In the 1980s, Russell Ackoff developed a process that he called interactive planning, which can be used in relation to the "unknown" future (Ackoff, 1981). Ackoff suggested that you had to create the organization's future, or others would do it for you, and then you would have to adapt to that created by others. Plan things yourself, or let others plan for you, was Ackoff's point. The idea behind research of future scenarios and the various methods associated with this is not so much to predict what will happen, but to offer various options, so that management can make their choices based on a broader range of information. In other words, it is the alternative and possible futures that should be anticipated, and an explanation of what these scenarios are based on. In this connection, system four will provide management with a useful tool that can be used when they are formulating decisions.

Whichever methods system four uses, and they should be aimed at dealing with information and assumptions concerning the system's environment. This information should then be explained, analysed and discussed before it is submitted to system five. It may be said that system four carries out a communication and information analysis of the external world around us so the whole organization constantly has sufficient knowledge to adapt to developments in the external world before changes manifest themselves as realities. In this way, the organization can function as a nimble and agile one, and have the ability to change before the market changes. This may be termed a type of early warning system. Such a warning system concerning critical variables in the environment should be developed and implemented by system four. By using an early warning system, the organization has an overview of development of the variables that are critical to the organization's survival (Van der Lans, 2012). To achieve this, system four must have the necessary expertise about how such early warning systems can be designed and implemented.

The point made by Beer, Ackoff, Boye (2011) and many others is that the responsibilities of system four are seldom developed as a separate function in organizations. This is where we believe HR departments can take on a new responsibility. This is also suggested by Armstrong (2014 2014a) and Ulrich (2013, 2013a), although they do not use Beer's theory or any other theory as a starting point. We stress in this chapter that if no one specifically responsible for carrying out the tasks we have outlined above, but instead everyone is responsible, then the responsibility will become pulverized. At worst, the tasks are not dealt with satisfactorily.

System four is termed "an eye on the future" precisely because this feature will ensure that the whole system has the necessary information, knowledge and insight about what will occur in relation to both short and long-term perspectives, for both the known and unknown futures.

Why is system four needed in relation to the HR department's future responsibilities? Firstly, there are few organizations today that have a function that takes care of the "eye on the future" (O'Reilly & Tushman, 2004; 2007; 2011; Thota & Munir, 2011). Secondly, there is no specific department in organizations that is responsible for driving innovation forward in small and medium sized businesses. Thirdly, system four functions as that part of an ambidextrous organization that ensures the autonomy of the organization as a whole. Fourthly, there is also no clear function in organizations that is responsible for developing and implementing early warning systems, systems for transfer of experience, idea-development and organizational learning. In this context, HR departments have a golden opportunity to become something other than a service function that in different ways trying to improve the working environment, by acting as the "merry minstrels" in an organization.

If these processes mentioned above, and the five areas of competence mentioned previously, are not dealt with as a specific function within an organization, the probability is high that the system's viability and survival will be at risk (O'Reilly & Tushman, 2004; 2007; 2011). In this context, the HR department has the potential to be take on a new function that has still not acquired its place in organizations, although many talk about the necessity of these processes being carried out (Armstrong, 2014; 2014a; Ulrich, 2013; 2013a). System four in Beer's theory and theory for viable organizations can in this context offer something innovative to ambidextrous organizations.

The need for the HR department taking on such a function as expressed here has been evident for a long period already. As early as 1982, the organizational theorist Kenyon Greene said the following: "A new explicitly recognized and project designed corporate level function will be required" (Greene, 1982: 36). Although he did not relate this new feature to system four or HR departments, he indicated that the external world was going to change so much in the future that organizations would need a new feature that explicitly planned for adapting to conditions in the external world.

With system four as a new functional area for HR departments, envisioning future scenarios will become an important new area of their expertise. This may be divided into two elements. One element is expectations, which is a passive element. Another element is creating an organization's future, which is an active element. The HR department can thus become a creative "factory" of an organization's future. The HR department is not a unit than makes decisions, but one that transmits expectations and information about the organization's future to system five, which is the highest decision-making unit. In this way, the organization's arena for learning, innovation and performance improvements will be greatly increased. System four is also important concerning the HR department's function as an arena for organizational learning.

This new function of the HR department is essential, because both transfer of experience and creative processes are necessary to promote innovation.

If these processes are not assigned to a functional area of the organization, then the organization will have difficulty in generating sufficient variation in relation to the external world (Ashby, 1956; Beer, 1995: 198; Schwaninger 2008), i.e. it will not meet the requirements regarding the law of "requisite variety" (Morgan, 2006: 109-110; Ashby, 1961; 1970; 1981).

Is there no one within the organization that is responsible for dealing with the above-mentioned functions? Beer answers: "In my experience, and not surprisingly, the man who usually gets the job (under whatever title) is the one who his colleagues think has the least chance of accomplishing change" (Beer, 1995: 242).

The point we are making here is that this responsibility should not be put in the hands of any short-term project, or single individual, who, for various reasons has been promoted within the organization beyond his/her expertise. Rather, the processes described should be the responsibility of a functional area of the organization that has already been established for this purpose. Beer's ideas expressed in 1995 are still applicable, which is apparent in the focus on ambidextrous organizations in recent research (McCarthy & Gordon, 2011; Thora & Munir, 2011; Chandrasekaren, 2012; Reinmoell & Reinmoeller, 2015; De Wit &

Meyer, 2014).

If an organization uses too much energy on maintaining internal stability, for example, by improving the working environment, and too little energy on knowledge processes, organizational learning, management of innovation, etc., then the organization will easily find itself in a position where it spends too much energy protecting its internal stability. This may maintain internal stability, but the changes in the external world will ultimately sweep the system away. When an organization uses too much time and resources on internal stability, this may result in a tendency to isolate itself from the outside world.

Conclusion

The problem for discussion in this chapter was: How can we design organizations to resolve the paradox of the co-existence of operational management (exploitation) and innovation (exploration).

This question can be answered by designing a new function into businesses. This function is described here as system four in Beer's theory.

One of the new functions for HR departments, assuming that they take over the functional areas represented by system four, will be to take responsibility for two key processes:

1. adapting the business to take account of changing external conditions; and
2. being important contributors to generating the future of the business.

Huber (1984), Drucker (1988; 1999; 1999a) and Morgan (1988; 1989; 1989a; 2006), present some interesting insights that support Beer's sustainability theory, and in particular our view here of the new function for HR departments. If we consider these insights in the context of Armstrong's (2014; 2014a) and White & Younger's, (2013:27-52) view concerning the future function of HR departments, we find an interesting theoretical implication regarding the new function of HR departments.

Drucker states quite clearly that centrally governed command and control theories will disappear and will be replaced by more effective governance systems (Drucker, 1988:45-53). This can be linked to system four's new position in businesses, together with the autonomous role occupied by system one in Beer's theory. Drucker also writes that it is extremely likely that self-governing groups with high levels of expertise in particular functional areas will be made responsible for resolving specialized assignments (Drucker, 1988; 1999; 1999a). Here these groups can be understood as specialists in a future HR function.

Huber's requirements for the future organization include a

requirement that future information processes regarding market innovations become more frequent and professionalized. According to Huber (1984), this professionalization will result in future organizational designs that favour innovative processes. It is here that we think Beer's theory, and in particular the new function for HR departments, may play a decisive role. We have found a similar approach in the research presentations of Armstrong (2014), White & Younger (2013), together with Ulrich (2013; 2013a); Ulrich, D. & Smallwood, N. (2006; 2007); Ulrich, et al., (2008); Ulrich, et al., (2008a); Ulrich, et al., (2012); Ulrich, et al., (2013); together with Ulrich & Ulrich, (2010).

Morgan's requirements for designs for future business structures are particularly prominent in "Organisasjonsbilder" [English: "Organizational images"](Morgan, 1988:89-110). Morgan's requirements are linked, among other things, to the co-existence of stability, flexibility and autonomy, something that is a key point in Beer's theory. Morgan (1988:89-110) imposes a further requirement on future organizations, namely that they must learn, adapt and change in step with changes in the surrounding world. In our opinion, this requirement is addressed by system four in Beer's theory.

Although Beer, Drucker, Morgan and Huber were writing about future organizations 15-30 years ago, it takes a long time for innovations, including organizational innovations, to be adopted in practice, and even longer for any particular innovation to become a dominant logic within the market. There is still a demand for theories that can give meaning to ambidextrous organizational design (Maier, 2015; Reinmoell & Reinmoeller, 2015; O'Reilley & Tushman, 2011).

According to Ulrich (2014; 2014a), and also White & Younger (2013), HR departments must be prepared to take responsibility for new tasks. This will require HR departments, to have a certain level of knowledge and competence in innovation management, knowledge management, change management, performance management and organizational design.

It is uncertain to what extent people with these competences will be found in-house, or whether small- and medium-sized businesses will resort to external consultants for this expertise. In the Norwegian context, where most business are small- or medium-sized, it seems reasonable to anticipate that businesses will hire in specialist expertise from the external market.

Further research

There is a need to identify the actual competences that a business needs to possess in order to adapt to the increasing pace of change, and increasingly complexity, in the surrounding world, and to generate its own future. We must also investigate whether HR departments working alone, or with the help of external specialists, can successfully acquire the competences that we have shown here to be necessary to meet the need for organizations to master the ambidextrous function of being simultaneously stable and flexible. At first sight, this may seem like a paradox, but a tightrope walker has to be simultaneously stable and flexible in order to reach his or her goal, which is the other end of the tightrope.

Index

ambidextrous, 16, 142, 143, 144, 145, 146, 151, 152, 156, 157, 159, 161, 162
analogy, 44, 48, 65
Analytical schemes, 48, 53, 66
Armstrong, 16
Asplund's motivation theory, 33, 34
attitudes, 19, 33, 45, 114, 133, 137, 97, 115
Balkan, 36
Bangalore, 32, 77, 135
Boudon-Coleman diagram, 3
36
Bunge, 137, 9, 25, 32, 35, 68, 79
bureaucratic, 26, 71, 72, 73, 116
capabilities, 14, 27, 28, 31, 36, 44, 47, 48, 54, 55, 56, 72, 70, 116
categories, 31, 33, 110, 38, 55
change, 12, 15, 22, 26, 27, 34, 37, 42, 50, 60, 68, 69, 71, 72, 73, 83, 86, 87, 88, 90, 91, 92, 93, 94, 95, 96, 98, 99, 100, 101, 103, 104, 105, 106, 107, 108, 109, 110, 129, 130, 134, 137, 145, 146, 149, 152, 154, 155, 157, 158, 161, 162, 68, 72, 92, 104, 113
Change management, 13, 15
change processes, 26, 37, 68, 72, 90, 94, 96
commitment, 21, 29, 30, 31, 91, 92, 109, 87
committed, 30, 132
communication, 21, 24, 32, 67, 71, 79, 127, 149, 155, 94
competence, 12, 13, 14, 15, 16, 19, 20, 21, 23, 25, 32, 34, 35, 36, 37, 58, 62, 63, 64, 67, 68, 70, 71, 72, 73, 76, 78, 79, 80, 81, 82, 83, 84, 85, 114, 116, 134, 135, 136, 137, 138, 141, 157, 161, 97
competition, 26, 28, 46, 62, 77, 81, 82, 83, 137
conceptual generalisation, 38, 39, 40, 42, 54, 65, 67
conceptual generalization, 12, 23, 28, 38
conceptual models, 39, 40, 41, 42, 43, 47, 48, 51, 53, 62, 63, 64, 65, 67
control, 24, 31, 34, 68, 101, 110, 112, 117, 135, 148, 149, 152, 160, 94, 120
cooperation, 28, 67, 73, 81, 82, 85, 136, 137
customers, 25, 28, 30, 37, 57, 58, 62, 70, 71, 72, 83, 84, 128
dedicated, 30, 127
emergence, 31, 42, 60, 130, 69, 80
Emergent, 9, 30

empirical generalisation, 38, 39
Feed-forward, 11
front line, 14, 25, 62, 64, 70, 71, 72, 73, 81, 84, 85
functional areas, 24, 26, 68, 70, 127, 159, 160
functional differentiation, 26
global, 14, 24, 26, 27, 28, 32, 34, 35, 36, 50, 60, 62, 63, 64, 67, 70, 72, 73, 76, 77, 78, 79, 80, 81, 82, 83, 84, 85, 116, 130, 133, 135, 136, 70, 72, 82, 114
Global communities, 35
global competence clusters, 32, 35, 70, 80, 84, 134, 135
globalization, 26, 31, 32, 34, 60, 64, 72, 76, 77, 80, 135, 136
Harvard model, 21
HR activities, 24, 32, 35
HR department, 20, 22, 25, 27, 30, 35, 37, 39, 118, 120, 122, 125, 137, 156, 157
HR departments, 16, 17, 21, 22, 24, 25, 26, 27, 28, 30, 31, 32, 33, 34, 35, 36, 37, 125, 136, 140, 142, 145, 146, 150, 152, 156, 157, 159, 160, 161, 162
HR- departments, 12, 16
HR function, 24, 35, 153, 160
HR functions, 24
HR managers, 40, 140
HR practices, 14, 24, 25, 27, 33, 39, 40, 41, 45, 51, 52, 54, 55, 56, 112, 113, 118, 135, 141, 123
HRM, 12, 13, 19, 20, 21, 22, 23, 24, 25, 26, 27, 29, 30, 31, 33, 34, 37, 39, 143, 75, 76, 81, 88, 91, 99, 102, 106, 107, 115, 123
HRM functions, 25, 34
HRM philosophy, 12, 19, 20, 22, 23, 25, 29, 30, 31, 33, 34, 37
HRM strategy, 13, 29, 39
HR-philosophy, 25
HR-policies, 25
HR-practices, 25
HR-processes, 25
HR-programmes, 25
human capital, 19, 33, 98
idea, 21, 35, 46, 67, 80, 81, 87, 91, 100, 123, 124, 125, 132, 141, 142, 155, 156
idea-development, 125, 156
identity, 20, 30, 64, 116, 70, 82

industrial society, 14, 31, 33, 34, 59, 60, 61, 64, 70, 72, 82, 111, 134
industrial workers, 34, 61, 77, 78, 111
infostructure, 14, 32, 36, 61, 62, 64, 66, 67, 68, 69, 70, 71, 76, 80, 81, 84, 85, 86, 125
infrastructure, 32, 36, 61, 67, 68, 69, 86
innovation, 16, 26, 32, 36, 37, 45, 48, 62, 67, 68, 70, 71, 72, 73, 76, 78, 80, 81, 83, 116, 124, 125, 126, 128, 132, 135, 136, 137, 139, 142, 143, 144, 149, 150, 156, 158, 159, 161, 52, 54, 58, 59, 82, 93, 94, 104, 105, 110, 120, 124
Innovation management, 13, 16
institutional theory, 31, 112
institutions, 22, 126, 136, 69
intangible, 29
interconnected, 27, 68, 112
international, 27, 32, 135, 75, 101, 111
Kahneman, 15, 31, 87, 90, 91, 92, 93, 94, 96, 97, 98, 99, 100, 101, 103, 104, 106, 107, 108, 82, 86, 88, 96, 97, 117
knowledge, 14, 15, 16, 19, 23, 25, 27, 29, 30, 31, 32, 33, 34, 35, 36, 37, 39, 40, 41, 44, 45, 47, 48, 49, 50, 52, 53, 54, 55, 56, 57, 58, 59, 60, 61, 63, 64, 66, 67, 68, 70, 71, 72, 73, 76, 77, 79, 80, 81, 82, 83, 84, 85, 101, 102, 105, 109, 111, 112, 113, 114, 115, 116, 117, 118, 119, 120, 121, 122, 123, 124, 126, 127, 128, 129, 130, 131, 132, 133, 135, 136, 137, 139, 140, 141, 146, 153, 155, 156, 159, 161, 39, 45, 53, 57, 58, 60, 62, 70, 76, 80, 82, 87, 89, 92, 94, 95, 98, 100, 102, 107, 111, 112, 113, 119, 123
knowledge economy, 34, 59, 72, 80, 116
Knowledge management, 13, 14, 111
knowledge organizations, 29, 57, 83, 112
knowledge processes, 60, 61, 81, 159
knowledge society, 19, 31, 32, 33, 34, 44, 59, 60, 61, 63, 64, 67, 68, 70, 71, 72, 73, 80, 82, 83, 85, 111, 131, 133, 146, 82, 94
knowledge workers' productivity, 15, 16, 111, 112, 113, 117, 139, 140, 141
knowledge-based organization, 14, 57, 58, 65, 84
law of requisite variety, 26, 33, 72
linear causal models, 46
management, 13, 14, 15, 16, 17, 19, 21, 24, 26, 27, 30, 31, 37, 39, 40, 41, 42, 43, 44, 45, 46, 48, 49, 50, 51, 52, 53, 54, 56, 63, 65,

66, 71, 84, 88, 91, 95, 96, 98, 101, 103, 104, 105, 106, 107, 109, 110, 112, 116, 118, 121, 122, 127, 129, 130, 131, 132, 133, 140, 142, 143, 144, 145, 149, 150, 152, 155, 159, 161, 51, 58, 73, 74, 84, 85, 89, 90, 91, 92, 93, 98, 99, 100, 104, 107, 108, 111, 112, 114, 116, 123, 124

measuring, 34, 42
Merton, 24
motivation, 21, 31, 33, 34, 82, 113, 130, 87, 90, 102, 115
multinational, 27
norms, 33, 148
North's action theory, 33, 34
Norths handlingsteori, 21
OECD, 12, 19
organization, 16, 19, 20, 22, 24, 26, 28, 29, 30, 31, 36, 37, 39, 46, 47, 48, 55, 56, 57, 58, 67, 68, 70, 72, 73, 76, 87, 96, 99, 107, 116, 121, 123, 125, 126, 127, 128, 129, 130, 138, 140, 141, 142, 143, 145, 146, 147, 149, 151, 152, 153, 154, 155, 156, 157, 158, 159, 160, 85, 91, 94, 112
organizational efficiency, 21
organizational learning, 73, 126, 156, 158, 159
organizations, 13, 14, 15, 17, 22, 24, 25, 26, 27, 32, 36, 39, 45, 47, 50, 54, 55, 56, 57, 61, 63, 64, 65, 68, 70, 71, 72, 81, 85, 86, 93, 95, 98, 99, 101, 105, 108, 112, 126, 138, 142, 144, 146, 147, 150, 152, 156, 157, 159, 161, 162, 73, 74, 84, 92, 104, 112, 115
outsourcing, 27, 32
pattern, 48, 133, 135, 38, 52, 62
performance, 14, 20, 21, 23, 36, 40, 41, 46, 51, 54, 55, 56, 57, 111, 112, 113, 114, 121, 123, 130, 131, 133, 137, 142, 143, 158, 161, 74, 75, 76, 83, 84, 88, 89, 91, 94, 97, 99, 102, 104, 106, 107, 115, 120, 123
Performance management, 13, 15
PESC, 27, 28, 29
phenomenon, 14, 42, 61, 64, 97, 135, 38, 42, 44, 45, 47, 49, 50, 51, 53, 54, 55, 58, 64, 67, 68
practitioners, 20
problem, 12, 15, 16, 37, 40, 42, 54, 86, 112, 113, 114, 116, 118, 139, 150, 159, 38, 39, 40, 42, 44, 45, 47, 49, 50, 51, 53, 54, 64, 67, 68, 70, 79

productivity, 16, 32, 34, 35, 63, 81, 111, 112, 113, 114, 115, 116, 117, 118, 119, 120, 121, 124, 126, 129, 133, 139, 140, 149, 51, 52, 59, 85, 94, 109, 123
promotions, 34
prospect theory, 15, 31, 86, 87, 90, 91, 92, 93, 94, 97, 98, 100, 109, 75
purpose, 16, 30, 42, 45, 47, 67, 136, 148, 158, 42, 47, 49, 52, 53, 54, 55, 61, 68, 81
reciprocity, 21
recruitment, 20, 23, 25, 34, 112
resource-based theory, 31
responsibility, 24, 25, 26, 27, 64, 107, 127, 128, 131, 149, 156, 158, 159, 161
reward, 23, 32, 104, 122
rules, 33, 88, 105, 148, 51, 112, 114
service, 35, 69, 71, 73, 119, 157, 99
strategic, 13, 14, 20, 21, 22, 24, 25, 27, 37, 39, 40, 41, 42, 43, 44, 45, 46, 49, 50, 51, 52, 53, 54, 56, 108, 128, 143, 73, 75, 84, 98, 99, 100, 108, 112, 114, 116, 123, 124
Strategic HRM, 12, 13, 142, 83, 102, 106, 107, 115, 123
strategic thinking, 24
suppliers, 25, 36, 37, 62, 70, 72
system, 24, 27, 28, 33, 40, 42, 51, 58, 62, 69, 73, 78, 81, 82, 85, 86, 97, 110, 112, 113, 118, 119, 122, 126, 128, 136, 147, 148, 149, 152, 153, 154, 155, 156, 157, 159, 160, 161, 39, 47, 51, 52, 53, 55, 56, 58, 65, 69, 72, 74, 76, 115
System four, 17, 149, 152, 153, 156, 157, 158
systemic approach, 39
talent, 24, 27, 29, 35, 36, 130
Thought experiments, 48, 50
Tversky, 15, 31, 87, 90, 91, 92, 97, 98, 99, 106, 108, 96, 97, 108, 117
typology, 13, 45, 49, 48, 52, 62, 63
value, 14, 29, 30, 35, 36, 40, 59, 61, 62, 63, 64, 65, 66, 68, 71, 73, 76, 80, 82, 83, 84, 85, 86, 120, 125, 126, 128, 148, 153, 73, 82, 113
values, 20, 30, 33, 148, 154, 96, 117
variation, 27, 55, 104, 158, 89

Chapter on concepts

Ambidextrous organizations. *Ambidextrous organizations* are organizations that have the ability to adapt to changes in external conditions while at the same time generating their own future by means of, among other things, performance improvement, growth and innovation (Duncan, 1976; O'Reilly & Tushman, 2004, 2006, 2011; Thota & Munir, 2011). In chapter 6, we have shown how ambidextrous organizations can be developed by HR departments.

In 2004, O'Reilly & Tushman expressed that ambidextrous organizations would constitute one of the major challenges for management in the global knowledge economy.

The findings of O'Reilly & Tushman (2004) were overwhelming. Regarding the launching of radical innovations, they found that none of the cross-functional or unsupported teams and only a quarter of the teams with functional designs were able to produce radical innovations. However, among the ambidextrous organizations, 90% were successful in producing radical innovations. Empirical research has shown that this type of organizational design is best for producing both incremental and radical innovations (Thora & Munir, 2011).

Asplund's motivation theory[7]. In brief, this theory can be described in the following way: *People are motivated by social responses* (Asplund, 2010: 221-229). The following statement may be said to be a central point made by Asplund's theory: *When people receive social responses, their level of activity increases.*

Asplund's motivation theory is consistent with North's action theory (ref. North's action theory). Understood in this way, it seems reasonable to connect the two theories in the statement: *People are motivated by the social responses rewarded by the institutional framework.*

---

[7] Asplund's motivation theory, a term we use here, is based on Asplund's research..

Availability cascades. This refers to the idea that we are all controlled by the image of reality created by the media, because this image is easy to retrieve from memory.

Availability proposition. This may be expressed as follow: The more easily information enters into our consciousness, the greater the likelihood that we will have confidence in that information. In other words, we believe more in the type of information that is available in memory than the information that is not so readily available.

Behavioural perspective. This perspective focuses on the behaviour of employees as an explanation for the relationship between business strategy and the results obtained.

Boudon-Coleman diagram. This research methodology was developed by Mario Bunge (Bunge, 1978:76-79) based on insights made by the sociologists Boudon and Coleman. The purpose of the diagram is to show the relationship between the various levels, such as the macro and micro-levels. For instance, it is shown how changes at the macro-level, such as technological innovations in feudal society, can lead to increased income at the micro-level. However, it was shown that technological innovations could lead to weakening of the semi-feudal structures because dependency on land owners was reduced. Consequently, the landowners opposed such changes especially in the case of technological innovations, which Boudon has shown in his research (Boudon, 1981: 100). Coleman (Coleman, 1990: 7-12) started at the macro level, went to the individual level to find explanations and finally ended up at the macro level again.

An important purpose of Bunge's Boudon-Coleman diagram is to identify social mechanisms that maintain or change the phenomenon or problem under investigation (as mentioned above, in Boudon's analysis of semi-feudal society). Bunge's Boudon-Coleman diagram may be said to represent a "mixed strategy"; Bunge says the following: *When studying systems of any kind a) reduce them to their components (at some level) and the interaction among these, as well as among them and environmental items, but acknowledge and explain emergence* (see the chapter on concepts) *whenever it occurs, and b) approach systems from all pertinent sides and on all relevant levels, integrating theories or even research fields whenever unidisciplinarity proves to be insufficient* (Bunge, 1998:78). The purpose of this research strategy is to arrive at a deeper and more complete explanation of a system's behaviour.

Capabilities. Capabilities are for an organization what abilities are for an individual.

An organizational capability may thus be defined as an organization's ability to perform a task, activity or process. Operational capabilities enable an organization to make money in the here and now (Winter, 2003: 991-995). Dynamic capabilities, as opposed to operational capabilities, are linked to processes of change. Change and innovation are at the centre of dynamic capabilities.

Simplified, one may say that organizational capabilities are something an organization does well compared to its competitors (Ulrich and Brockbank, 2005). These capabilities are intangible and therefore difficult for competitors to imitate (Wernerfelt, 1984).

Cohesive energy. In a social system cohesive energy is "the glue" that binds the system together. Cohesive energy is the social mechanisms that make the system durable. According to systemic thinking it is the relationships and actions that bind social systems together. The rationale is that relationships and the systems of relationships may be said to control human behaviour. Social systems are held together (in systemic thinking) by dynamic social relations (e.g. feelings, perceptions, norms) and social action (e.g. cooperation, solidarity, conflict and communication).

Co-creation. Co-creation involves working together to promote knowledge processes and innovation. If knowledge processes and innovation are essential for value creation in the knowledge society, co-creation is an important social mechanism for initiating, maintaining and strengthening these processes. The balance between competition and cooperation, embodied in the concept of co-creation, leads to constructive criticism and the necessary scope of knowledge that exists in the network so as to promote creativity and the innovative. Instead of a zero-sum situation, a positive-sum situation will be developed where everyone wins.

Collective blindness. Collective blindness may be said to be a form of collective arrogance, which results in irrational actions. Minor events slip under the radar, causing the system to not be fully aware of what is happening. Politicians' explanations why voters in a referendum vote contrary to what most of the power elite and the media advocated is an example of collective blindness.

Competence. Competence refers to knowledge, skills and attitudes.

Core Competence. The concept was popular in the strategy literature of the 1990s. Core competence may be defined as: *"a bundle of skills and technologies that enable a company to provide a particular benefit to customers"* (Hamel & Prahalad, 1996:219). More recently, core competence as a concept has been given less attention in the research on dynamic capabilities, and now there is more focus on the concept of *fitness*. The term *evolutionary fitness* is also used in the research literature in connection with technology, quality, cost development, market development, innovation and competitive positioning (Helfat, et al, 2007: 7).

Discontinuous innovations. These are innovations that change the premises of technology, markets, our mindset, and so on. We know that sooner or later discontinuous innovations will emerge in the future (Hewing, 2013).

Dynamic capabilities. Dynamic capabilities stem from the resource-based perspective and evolutionary thinking in strategy literature (Teece, 2013: 3-65; 82-113; Nelson and Winter, 1982). The dynamic perspective attempts to explain what promotes an organization's competitive position over time through innovation and growth (Teece, 2013: x).

The original thinking concerning dynamic capabilities may be related to Teece et al. (1997). These authors defined dynamic capabilities as *an organization's ability to create, develop and modify its internal and external expertise in order to address changes in the external world.*

Dynamic capabilities are now seen as all the organizational processes, not only internal and external expertise, that contribute to an organization's capacity to adapt to change while creating the organization's future.

Explicit knowledge. This is knowledge that can be digitized and communicated to others as information.

Evidence. This may be results, such as research results, that can be relied on. However, it is also important to be aware of the fact that other evidence may be available without having to refer to figures and quantities, such as evidence that emerges from observations and good judgment without the assessment being quantified. Evidence-based research is research results that are based on approved and accepted scientific research methods.

Emergent. An emergent occurs if something new turns up on one level that has not previously existed on the level below. With emergent we mean: *Let S be a system with composition A, i.e. the various components in addition to the way they are composed. If P is a property of S, P is emergent with regard to A, if and only if no components in A possess P; otherwise P is to be regarded as a resulting property with regards to A.* (Bunge, 1977:97).

Entrepreneurial spirit. The entrepreneurial spirit may be described as follows (Roddick, 2003: 106-107):

- The vision of something new and belief in this that is so strong that belief becomes reality.
- A touch of positive madness.
- The ability to stand out from the crowd.
- Creative tension bubbling over.
- Pathological optimism.
- To act before you know!
- Basic desire for change.
- Creative energy focused on ideas, not on explicit factual knowledge.
- Being able to tell the story you want to sell.

Feedback Giving the other person feedback, for instance with regard to their behaviour, attitudes, and the like, is the most important element in the area of interactive skills and emotional intelligence (Goleman, 1996; 2007). Analysis of feedback is a sure way to identify our strengths and then reinforce them (Wang, et al., 2003). Failure to give people feedback on their behavior in some contexts may even be considered immoral.

Feed-forward. Feed-forward is regarded here as an expectation mechanism. It seems reasonable to assume that our expectations influence our behaviour in the present. It is therefore important that we make explicit to ourselves the expectations we have of a situation. By making expectations explicit, we have a greater opportunity to learn from our experiences and thus improve our performance.

Front line focus. This refers to those in the front line, i.e. in direct contact with customers, users, patients, students, etc. They have the greatest expertise, necessary information, and decision-making authority and are regarded as the most important resource in the organization because they are at the point where an organization's value creation occurs.

Global competence network. These competence networks may be divided into political, social, economic, technological and cultural patterns. It is when these five patterns interact that one may perceive the overall pattern. In the global knowledge economy it seems reasonable to assume that those who control this pattern set the conditions for economic development. These global competence networks will most likely make an impact on HR departments in companies competing for this kind of expertise in national markets.

Global competence networks are also emphasized as crucial for economic growth by OECD (2001), although they use the term *innovative clusters.* The purpose of innovative clusters and global competence networks is the development, dissemination and use of new ideas that promote wealth creation.

There is much to suggest that a greater degree of integration and cooperation between private and public sectors at the national and regional levels is an important prerequisite for initiating the innovative locomotive effect. The global competence networks are metaphorically the energy source that sustains the motion of this locomotive. It would be counterproductive to replace the locomotive once in motion. Conversely, the individual carriages of the locomotive (read: organizational level) can be changed depending on their competitive position. The individual passengers on the train create ideas and knowledge through the processes that may be called *creative chaos*. In this way we will arrive at a tripartite of the prerequisites for global competence networks. At the individual level, creative chaos occurs. At the organizational level, there will be creative destruction. At the social and global levels, creative collaboration takes place. These three processes create innovation and economic growth as an emergent, not as a *future perfectum*, i.e. a planned process with given results.

A prerequisite for the reasoning above is that tension and competition at one level requires collaboration at another level. Competition and cooperation are both necessary if one is to develop innovation and economic growth, in the same manner that stability and change are necessary for flexibility. Too much of the one (stability) leads to rigidity, and too much of the other (change) leads to chaos. Understood in this way, emergents cannot be planned.

Hamel's Law of Innovation. The "law" states that only between one and two of one thousand ideas become innovations in a market (Hamel, 2002; 2012). Therefore, an infostructure must be created to ensure that ideas are continuously produced in a business.

Hidden knowledge. Hidden knowledge is what we do not know we do not know. Kirzner (1982) says that hidden knowledge is possibly the most important knowledge domain of creativity, innovation and entrepreneurship.

History's "slow fields".

This refers to the fact that norms, values and actions tend to be in operation long after the functions, activities and processes that initially created them disappear, thus generating so-called *slow fields of history*. These norms, values and actions exist though they have no apparent function, contributing to maintaining a type of behaviour long after the type of behaviour is functional or meaningful[8]. For sociologists and historians it is important to determine whether norms and values have any function, or whether they are part of history's slow fields. By examining history's slow fields, it may be possible to provide better explanations for phenomena.

HR management. HR management is defined as HR practices at various levels (micro, meso, macro) for managing people in organizations.

HR management has been defined in many different ways. For instance, Boxall and Purcell (2003:1) define HR management as all those activities oriented towards managing relations between employees in an organization. This definition emphasizes the relational perspective. Later, they expanded their definition to include all the activities and processes that underpin an organization's value creation (Boxall and Purcell, 2010:29). On

---

[8] Asplund (1970: 55) refers to a similar phenomenon when he discusses Simmel. He points out that the norms that may have had a positive function during a historic phase become in a later phase dysfunctional.

this basis, Armstrong defines the activities and processes that HR management should engage in: *"HRM covers activities such as human capital management, knowledge management, organizational design and development, resource planning (recruitment, talent development), performance management, organizational learning, reward systems, relationships between employees, and employees' wellness."* (Armstrong, 2014:6). However, we believe Armstrong underestimates two essential areas of knowledge in his definition: the management of innovation processes, and change processes in organizations. Innovation and change are strongly emphasized in the global HRM Survey (White & Younger, 2013:35-39). Armstrong has included the ethical perspective in his Handbook for HRM (Armstrong, 2014a:95-105). Management of innovation processes and change processes in organizations is also highlighted and underlined by Wright et al. (2011: 5) in their description of HRM. However, it must also be said that Armstrong discusses innovation (Armstrong, 2014:145-155), but not in his process definition of HR management. Innovation and change processes are also emphasized by Ulrich et al. (2013). Brockbank (2013: 24) especially mentions these two processes as being important in the research model Ulrich et al. (2013) have developed through their empirical research over 25 years.

Implicit Knowledge. This is knowledge that is spread throughout an organization but not integrated.

Information input overload. This occurs when an individual, a team, an organization or a community receive more information than they can manage to process.

In a situation characterised by information input overload the following may occur (Miller, 1978: 123):

1. Designated tasks and responsibilities are left undone
2. Errors are made
3. Queues of information occur
4. Information is filtered out that should have been included

5. Abstract formulations are made when they should have been specific
6. Communication channels are overloaded, creating stress and tension in the system
7. Complex situations are shunned
8. Information is lumped together for processing

Each of the above eight points may result in a decrease in efficiency when the system is exposed to information input overload.

Infostructure. The infostructure concerns the processes that enable the development, transfer, analysis, storage, coordination and management of data, information and knowledge. The infostructure consists of eleven generic processes, as shown in Fig. 8 in this book. The eleven processes in the infostructure may be considered as nodes in a social network at different levels, for example team, organization, society, and region, all in the global space. Together, the eleven processes comprise the totality of the infostructure.

It may be said that the *info*structure has the same importance in the knowledge society as the *infra*structure had in the industrial society.

Innovation. Innovation is here understood as any idea, practice or material element, which is perceived as new for the person using it (Zaltman et al., 1973).

Ideas are seen as the smallest unit in the innovation process (Hamel, 2002; 2012). However, this refers to the ideas that are in process of development and not fully developed ideas. Before an idea can be characterized as innovative, it must prove to be beneficial to somebody, i.e. the market must accept the idea and apply it. Consequently, the creative process of innovation is here understood as the benefit it has for a market (Amabile, 1990; Johannessen, et al., 2001: 25). Thus, it is not sufficient that an idea is new for it to be considered an innovation. An idea may have a great degree of novelty, but if it is of no benefit to anybody in the market, then it has no innovative value.

Kaizen. This is a Japanese method, which means that an organization develops systems for organized improvement (Maurer, 2012).

Knowledge. The definition of knowledge used here is *the systematization and structuring of information for one or more goals or purposes.*

Knowledge worker. A knowledge worker has been described by the OECD as *a person whose primary task is to generate and apply knowledge*, rather than to provide services or produce physical products (OECD, 2000 a, b, c, d, e; 2001). This may be understood as a *formal definition* of a knowledge worker.

This definition does not restrict knowledge workers to creative fields, as is the case with, for example, Mosco and McKercher (2007: vii–xxiv). The OECD definition also allows for the fact that a knowledge worker may perform routine tasks. The definition also does not limit the type of work performed by knowledge workers to tasks relating to creative problem-solving strategies, unlike the definition provided by Reinhardt et al. (2011).

Knowledge enterprise. This is an enterprise that has knowledge as its most significant output. It is perhaps helpful to think of the process *input - process - output* to separate industrial enterprises from knowledge enterprises. Much knowledge and skills are needed to produce high-tech products such as computers, and there are also many knowledge workers involved in this process. However, the majority of products produced today are high-tech industrial products, and although such products require very skilled knowledge in the production process, they are nevertheless output-industrial products.

On the other hand, law firms, consulting firms and universities are examples of knowledge enterprises.

Knowledge management. Management of knowledge resources

in an organization. These resources may be explicit knowledge, implicit knowledge, tacit knowledge and hidden knowledge.

Locomotive effect. This refers to something that generates and then reinforces an activity or development.

Modularization. An extreme fragmentation of the production process in the global knowledge economy. Production is fragmented and distributed according to the following logic: Costs – quality – competence – design – innovation.

Modular flexibility. The modulization of value creation. Modular flexibility may best be understood as the globalization of production processes, and extreme specialization of work processes with a focus on core processes.

Necessary and sufficient conditions. It may often be appropriate to divide conditions or premises into *necessary conditions* and *sufficient conditions*. Necessary conditions must be present to trigger an action, but these may not be sufficient. The sufficient conditions must also be present to trigger the action.

North's action theory[9]. This action theory may be expressed in the following statement: *People act on the basis of a system of rewards as expressed in the norms, values, rules and attitudes in the culture (the institutional framework)* (North, 1990; 1993*)*. North's action theory is also consistent with Asplund's motivation theory (ref. Asplund's motivation theory).

Primary task. An organization's primary task is what the system is designed to do.

Proposition. This is an overarching hypothesis. It says something about the relationship between several variables. A proposition relates to a hypothesis in the same way the main research problem

---

[9] North's action theory is a term we use here based on North's research.

relates to research questions.

Punctuation. By punctuation (Bateson, 1972:292-293) a distinction is drawn between cause and effect; this is done with a clear motive in mind. A causality is thus created which does not actually exist in the real world, and one is then free to discuss the effects of this cause which has been created through a process of punctuation.

A sequence of a process is selected, and then bracketed. In this way, we de-limit what is punctuated from the rest of the process. Figuratively, we may imagine this as a circle that is divided into small pieces; one piece of the circle is then selected and folded out into a straight line. This results in the creation of an artificial beginning and end. This beginning and end of course cannot exist in a circle, but only through the process of punctuation.

Social laws. Social laws constitute a pattern of a unique type. They are systemic and connected to a system of knowledge, and cannot change without the facts they represent also being changed (Bunge, 1983; 1983a). The main differences between a statement of a law and other statements are:

1. Law statements are general.

2. Law statements are systemic, i.e. they are related to the established system of knowledge.

3. Law statements have been verified through many studies.

A pattern may be understood as variables that are stable over a specific period of time. A social law is created when an observer gains insight into the pattern. By gaining such insight, we can also predict parts of behaviour or at least develop a rough estimate within a short period of time.

Social laws are further related to specific social systems, both in time and space. However, this does not represent any objection to social laws, because this is also true of natural laws (although these have a longer time span and are of a more general nature).

Social mechanism. Robert Merton (1967) brought the notion of social mechanisms into sociology, although we can find rudiments of this in both Weber – with the Protestant ethic as an explanation for the emergence of capitalism in Europe – and in Durkheim, who uses society as an explanation for a rising suicide rate. For Merton, social mechanisms are the building blocks of *middle range theories*. He defines social mechanisms as *social processes having designated consequences for designated parts of the social structure* (Merton, 1968:43). In the 1980s and 1990s, Jon Elster developed a new notion of the role of social mechanisms in sociology (Elster, 1983;1989). Hedstrom and Swedberg write that, *the advancement of social theory calls for an analytical approach that systematically seeks to explicate the social mechanisms that generate and explain observed associations between events* (Hedstrøm & Swedberg, 1998:1).

It is one thing to point out connections between phenomena. It is something quite different to point out satisfactory explanations for these relationships, which is what social mechanisms accomplish. A social mechanism tells us what will happen, how it will happen and why it will happen (Bunge, 1967). Social mechanisms are primarily analytical constructs which cannot necessarily be observed; in other words, they are epistemological, not ontological. However, social mechanisms are observable in their consequences. An intention can be a social mechanism of action. We cannot observe an intention, but we can interpret it in light of the consequences manifested through an action. Preferences can also function as a social mechanism for economic behaviour. We cannot observe a person's preferences, but we can interpret them in the light of the behavioural consequences that manifest themselves. Social mechanisms are, understood in this way, analytical constructs, indicating connections between events (Hernes, 1998).

Bunge says: *"... a social mechanism is a process in a concrete system, such that it is capable of being about or preventing some change in the system as a whole or in some of its subsystems"* (Bunge, 1997:414). By 'social mechanism' here we mean those activities that promote/inhibit social processes in relation to a specific problem / phenomenon.

Material resources and technology are social mechanisms of the economic subsystem; power is a social mechanism of the political subsystem; fundamental norms and values are a social mechanism of the cultural subsystem; and human relationships are a social mechanism of the social subsystem. These system-specific social mechanisms interact with each other to achieve certain goals, maintain these systems, or to avoid certain undesirable conditions in the system or the outside world.

The difficulty of discovering social mechanisms and distinguishing them from processes may be partly explained by the fact that social mechanisms are also processes (Bunge, 1997:414). For the application of social mechanisms, see the Boudon-Coleman diagram.

Social system. From a systemic perspective, social systems can be conceptual or concrete. Theories and analytical models are examples of conceptual systems. Further, social systems are *composed of people and their artifacts* (Bunge, 1996:21). Social systems are held together (in systemic reasoning) by **dynamic**

social relations (such as emotions, interpretations, norms, etc.) and **social actions** (such as, cooperation, solidarity, conflict and communication, etc.). None of the social actions have precedence in the systemic interpretation of social systems, such as conflict in the case of Marx, and solidarity in the case of Durkheim.

Staccato-behaviour (erratic behaviour). If organizations introduce too many change processes in succession too quickly, a phenomenon may occur called "staccato-behaviour".

If an organization does not deal with this appropriately, it seems reasonable to assume that workers will become tired, burnt-out and de-motivated. Perhaps most damaging to business, employees will lose focus on their primary task - what the business is designed to do. In addition, businesses will often experience that this leads to an increasing degree of opportunistic behaviour (Ulrich, 2013a:260).

Strategic HR management. Strategic HR management is defined in this book as: *The choices an HR department makes with regard to human resources for the purposes of achieving the organization's goals.* This is analogous to the view of Storey et al. (2009:3) and consistent with the definition we employ of HR management. This means that strategic HR management must be focused on the *micro, meso* and *macro-levels.*

There are many definitions of strategic HR management. For instance, *use of human resources in order to achieve lasting competitive advantages for the business* (Mathis and Jackson, 2008:36); *management of the employees, expressed through management philosophy, policy and praxis* (Torrington et al., 2005:28); *development of a consistent practices in order to support the strategic goals of the business* (Mello, 2006:152); *a complex system with the following characteristics: vertical integration, horizontal integration, efficiency, partnership* (Schuler and Jackson, 2005).

Systemic thinking. Systemic thinking makes a distinction between the epistemological sphere (Bunge, 1985), the ontological sphere

(Bunge, 1983), the axiological sphere (Bunge, 1989, 1996) and the ethical sphere (Bunge, 1989). Systemic thinking makes a clear distinction between intention and behaviour. Intention is something that should be *understood*, while behaviour is something that should be *explained*. To understand an intention we must study the historical factors, situations and contexts, as well as the expectation mechanisms. Behaviour must be explained with respect to the context, relationships and situation it unfolds in. What implication does the distinction between intention and behavior have for the study of social systems?

Interpretation of meaning is an important part of the *intention aspect* in the distinction. Explanation and prediction become an essential part of the *behavioral aspect* of the distinction.

In systemic thinking it is the link between the interpretation of meaning and explanation, and prediction, which provides historical and social sciences with practical strength. By making a distinction between intention and behaviour, the historical and the social sciences are interpretive, explanatory and predictive projects. According to systemic thinking, many of the contradictions in the historical and social sciences spring from the fact that a distinction is not made between intention and behaviour. The problem of the historical and social sciences is that the actors who are studied have both intentions and they also exercise types of behaviour; however, this isn't problematic as long as we make a distinction between intention and behaviour. By simultaneously introducing the distinction between intention and behaviour, systemic thinking has made it possible to identify, for instance, partial explanations from each of two main epistemological positions, namely, the naturalists and anti-naturalists (Johannessen & Olaisen, 2005; 2006), and synthesize these explanations into new knowledge.

Systemic thinking emphasizes circular causal processes, also called *interactive causal processes*, in addition to linear causal processes (Johannessen, 1996; 1997). Systemic thinking argues that to understand objective social facts, one must examine the subjective aspects of these. In systemic thinking, objective social facts exist, but they are often more difficult to grasp than facts in the natural world, because social facts are often influenced by expectations, emotions, prejudices, ideology and economic and social interests.

"Aspect-seeing" is thus a way of approaching these social facts.

Emergents are central to systemic thinking. A pattern behind the problem or phenomenon is always sought in systemic investigations. Patterns may be revealed by studying the underlying processes that constitute a phenomenon or problem, *and the search for pattern is what scientific research is all about* (Bunge, 1996:42).

According to systemic thinking it is a misconception to say that the facts are social constructions. The misunderstanding involves confusing our *concepts* concerning facts and our *hypotheses* about the facts together with the facts. Our concepts and hypotheses are mental constructs. The facts, however, are not mental constructs. Social need, for instance, is not a social fact; it is a mental construct of, for instance, starvation. Starvation is a social fact. Social need is a mental or social construction. Not being able to read is a social fact. Illiteracy is, however, a social construction.

A *symbol* should symbolize something, just as a *concept* should delineate something. A *hypothesis* should explain something or express something about relationships. A conceptual *model* should say something about the relationships between concepts. A *theory* should say something about relationships between propositions. Physical or social facts are untouched by all these mental constructions. That one can through constructs change social facts, or that social facts are changed as a social consequence of using constructs, is neither original nor new.

The aim of theoretical research, according to the systemic position, is the construction of systems, i.e. theories (Bunge, 1974: v). The order in systemic research is thus: Theory - Analysis - Synthesis.

In the methodological sphere, the systemic position has its main focus on relationships, both in terms of concrete things, ideas and knowledge. Consequently, systemic thinking encourages interdisciplinary and multidisciplinary approaches to problems or phenomena.

The systemic position thus attempts to bridge the gap between methodological individualism and methodological collectivism, which is considered the classic controversy in historical- and social sciences.

The perceptions that an observer has about social systems will influence his/her actions, regardless of whether the perceptions are true or fallacious. Systemic investigations start, therefore, writes Bunge *from individuals embedded in a society that preexists them and watch how their actions affect society and alter it* (Bunge, 1996:241). The study of social systems from a systemic perspective for these reasons always includes the triad: actors - observers - social systems.

The observer tries to uncover a system's composition, environment and structure. Then the actors' subjective perception of composition, environment and structure are examined. In other words, both the subjective and objective aspects are studied. When we wish to study changes in social systems, from a systemic point of view, we have to examine the social mechanisms (drivers) that influence changes; both internal and external social mechanisms must be identified. This study takes place within the four subsystems: the economic, political, cultural and relational.

According to systemic thinking, social changes occur along seven axes:

1. As an *expectation* of new relationships, values, power constellations, technologies and distribution of material resources.
2. As a result of our *beliefs* (mental models) about relationships, values, power constellations, technical and material resources.
3. As a result of *psychological elements*, such as: irritation, crisis, discomfort, unsatisfactory life, unworthy life, loss of well-being, etc.
4. As a result of *communication* in and between systems.
5. As a result of an *understanding of connections* (contextual understanding).
6. As a result of learning and new *self-knowledge*.
7. As a result of *new ideas* and ways of thinking.

Historiography, from a systemic perspective, has one clear goal: to investigate what happened, where it happened, when it happened, how it happened, why it happened, and with what results.

Systemic assumptions related to historiography and social sciences may be expressed in the following (Bunge 1998:263):

a. The past has existed.

b. Parts of the past can be known.

c. Every uncovering of the past will be incomplete.

d. New data, techniques, and systemizations and structuring will reveal new aspects of the past.

e. Historical knowledge is developed through new data, discoveries, hypotheses and approaches.

In systemic thinking if changes are to take place, then the material will sometimes be given precedence; at other times, ideology, ideas and thinking are given precedence. In other contexts, there is a systemic link between the material and ideas that is needed to bring about changes. In such contexts, it is difficult and irrelevant to say what is the primary driver, i.e. the material or ideas; this would be on par with discussing what came first, the chicken or the egg.

The processes that drive social change, according to a systemic perspective, are the interaction between the economic, political, relational and cultural subsystems. In some situations, one of these four perspectives will prevail, whereas in others it will be one or more of the four subsystems that are the drivers of social change. In many cases, it is precisely the interaction between the four subsystems that leads to social changes.

In this context the systemic perspective may be described by saying that material conditions/energy, such as economic relationships, may provide the ground from which ideologies develop, but that these ideologies in return influence the development of the material. Whether material conditions / energy or ideology comes first is often determined by a historiographical punctuation process (Bateson, 1972:163).

The systemic perspective balances historical materialism and historical idealism. It assumes that overall social changes are the result of economic, political, social and cultural factors, in addition to the interaction between material conditions / energy and ideas. Furthermore, a systemic perspective views any society as being interwoven into its surroundings (Bunge, 1998: 275). When a historian considers a historical situation – such as the massacre in Van in April 1915 – from this perspective then he is trying *to throw light upon the internal working of a past culture and society* (Stone, 1979: 19).

The systemic position attempts to view the relevant event in a larger context, in order to find *the patterns which combine* (Bateson, 1972:273-274), because *change depends upon feedback loop* (Bateson, 1972:274). Bunge says about this position: *By placing the particular in a sequence, adopting a broad perspective the systemist overcomes the idiographic/nomothetic duality, ..., as well as the concomitant narrative/structural opposition* (Bunge 1998:275). This means, metaphorically, that the systemic researcher uses a microscope, telescope and a helicopter to investigate patterns over time.

Systemic research strategy is a *zig-zagging between the micro-meso and macro levels* (Bunge, 1998:277). Through a systemic research strategy the researcher has ample opportunities to use a Boudon-Coleman diagram.

Systemic thinking examines four types of changes[10].

Type I change concerns individuals who change history, such as Genghis Khan, Hitler, Stalin, Mao Zedong, etc.

Type II change concerns groups of people acting together who change history. Examples of Type II change include the invasion of the Roman Empire by peoples from the north; and the Ottoman expansion into the Balkans between the late 1400s and when the Ottoman Empire was pushed back partly due to nationalist liberation movements in the early 1900s.

Type III change include changes in history that are caused by natural disasters, such as the volcanic eruption that destroyed Pompeii. Climate change may also be said to an example of a type III change.

Type IV change involves a total change in the way of thinking, such as the emergence of new religions, like Islam, or a new political ideology, such as Marxism.

---

[10] The four types of changes are related to Bateson's (1972:279-309) work on different types of learning, especially those discussed in his article *Logical types of learning and communication*.

The systemic researcher attempts to explore the relationship between the four types of changes. A single event is in itself not necessarily of special interest to the systemic researcher; rather, the focus is on the *system of events* of which the single event is a part.

All the social sciences are used in the systemic position to seek insight, understanding and to explain a phenomenon or problem.

Tacit knowledge. Knowledge that is difficult to communicate to others as information. It is also very difficult, if at all possible, to digitize.

The knowledge-based perspective. The knowledge-based perspective is defined here as creating, expanding and modifying internal and external competencies to promote what the organization is designed to do (Grant, 2003: 203).

The resource-based perspective. This perspective can be defined as the structuring and systematization of the organization's internal *resources* so it is difficult for competitors to copy them.

Theory. Here understood as a system of propositions (Bunge, 1974: v).

References

Abercrombie,N.; Hill, S. & Turner, B. (1984). Dictionary of Sociology, Penguin, Harmondsworth.

Acemoglu, D. (2003). Labor-and Capital-Augmenting Technical Change, Journal of European Economic Association, 1, 1:1-37.

Ackoff, R.L. (1981). Creating the Corporate Future: Plan or be Planed for, John Wiley & Sons, London.

Adler, P.; Goldoftas, B. & Levine, D. (1999). Flexibility versus Efficiency? A Case Study of Model Changeovers in the Toyota Production System, Organizational Science, 10:43-68.

Adner, R. & Helfat, C. (2003). Corporate effects and dynamic managerial capabilities, Strategic Management Journal, 24:1011-1026.

Adriaenssen, D. & Johannessen, J-A. (2015). Conceptual

generalisation: Methodological reflections in social science a systemic viewpoint, Kybernetes, 44, 4: 588-605.

Albrow, M. (1999). The global age, Stanford University Press, CAL.

Alveson, M. (2000). Social identity and the problem of lojality in knowledge intensive companies, Journal of Management Studies, 37,8:1101-1123.

Amabile, T. (1990). Within you, without you: The social psychology of creativity, and beyond, in Runco, M.A.; Albert, R.S. (eds.). Theories of creativity, Sage, London. S. 61-91.

Appelbaum, E. & Batt, R. (1994). The New American Workplace, Cornell University Press, Ithaca, NY.

Armstrong, M. (2014). Armstrong's Handbook of Strategic Human Resource Management, Kogan Page, New York.

Armstrong, M. (2014a). Armstrong's Handbook of Human Resource Management Practice, Kogan Page, New York.

Arrow, K. (1951). Alternative approaches to the theory of choice in risk-taking situations, Econometrica, 19:404-437.

Ashby, W.R. (1945). Effect of Controls on Stability, Nature, vol.155,24. February.

Ashby, W.R.(1961). An Introduction to Cybernetics, Chapman & Hall LTD, New York.

Ashby, W.R. (1970). Connectance of Large Dynamic (Cybernetic) Systems: Critical Values for Stability. Nature, Vol 228 no. 5273 Nov. 21.

Ashby, W.R. (1981). What is an Intelligent Machine? In Conant, R. (Ed.), Mechanisms of Intelligence. California: Intersystems Seaside.

Asplund, J. (1970). Om undran innför samhället, Argos, Stockholm.

Asplund, J. (2010). Det sociala livets elementära former, Korpen, Stockholm

Axford, B. (1995). The global system: Economics, politics and culture, Polity Press, Cambridge.

Autor, D.; Levy, F. & Murnane, R.J. (2003). The Skill Content of recent technological change: An empirical exploration, The Quarterly Journal of Economics, Vol. 118, no. 4, pp. 1279-1333.

Azmat, G.; Manning, A. & Van Reenen, J. (2012). Privatization and the Decline of the Labour's Share: International Evidence from Network Industries, Economica, 79:470-492.

Baird, L. & Henderson, J.C. (2001). The Knowledge Engine, Berrett-Koehler, San Francisco.

Barney, J.B. & Clark, D.N. (2007). Resource-Based Theory: Creating and sustaining Competitive Advantage, OUP, Oxford.

Bailey, K.D. (1990). Social Entropy Theory, State University New York Press, Albany.

Bailey, K.D. (1994). Sociology and the New Systems Theory: Towards a Theoretical Synthesis, State University of New York Press, Albany.

Bailey, K.D. (2006). Systems Theory, in Jonathan H. Turner, Handbook of Sociological Theory, Springer, New York. S. 379-405.

Bailey, M.T. (1992). Do Physicists Use Case Studies? Public Administration Review, 52, 1:47-54.

Bateson, G. (1972). Steps to an ecology of mind, Ballantine Books, New York.

Bateson, G. (1988). Ande och Natur, Symposion Bokförlag, Stockholm.

Barney, J.B. (1991). Firm Resources and sustained competitive advantage, Journal of Management, 17, 1:99-120.

Barney, J.B. (1995). Looking inside for competitive advantage, Academy of Management Executive, 9, 4:49-61.

Barney, J.B. (2001). Is the resource based view a useful perspective for strategic management research? Yes, Academy of Management Review, 26:41-56.

Barney, J.B. & Clark, D.N. (2007). Resource-Based Theory:

Creating and Sustaining Competitive Advantage, Oxford University Press, Oxford.

Bauman, Z. (1992). Intimitations of postmodernity, Routledge, London.

Bauman, Z. (2011). Culture in a liquid modern world, Polity Press, London.

Barnard, C. I. (1974). The Functions of the Excecutive, Harvard University Press, Boston.

Beach, L.R. & Connolly, T. (2005). The psychology of decision making: People in organizations, Sage, London.

Becker, B.E.; Huselid, M.A.; Pickus, P.S. & Spratt, M.F. (1997). HR as a source of shareholder value:research and recommendations, Human Resource Management, 36, 1:39-48.

Becker, B.E. & Huselid, M.A. (1998). High Performance Work Systems and firm performance: A Synthesis of research and managerial implications. I Ferris, G.R. (Red.). Research in personnel and human resources management, JAI Press, Greenwich. S. 53-101.

Beer, M.; Spector, B.; Lawrence, P.R.; Quinn Mills, D. & Walton, R.E. (1984). Managing Human Assets: The Groundbreaking Harvard Business School Program, The Free Press, New York.

Beer, S. (1979). The heart of enterprise: John Wiley & Sons,

Chichester.

Beer, S. (1981). Brain of the Firm, John Wiley & Son, New York.

Beer, S. (1995). Diagnosing the system for organizations, John Wiley & Sons, London.

Bennis, W.G.; Cloke, K. & Goldsmith, J. (2012). The End of Management and the Rise of Organizational Democracy, John Wiley & Sons, New York.

Berger, P. (1987). The capitalist revolution: Fifty propositions about prosperity, equality and liberty, Basic Books, New York.

Bicak, K. (2005). International Knowledge Transfer Management, Shaker Verlag, Aachen.

Bishop, C.M. (2007). Pattern Recognition and machine Learning, Springer, Berlin.

Bledow, R.; Frese, M.; Anderson, N.; Erez, M. & Farr, J. (2009). A Dialectic Perspective on Innovation: Conflicting Demands, Multiple Pathways, and Ambidexterity, Industrial and Organizational Psychology, Perspectives on Science and Practice, 2, 3:305-337.

Boettcher, W.A. (2004). The prospects for prospect theory: An empirical evaluation of international relations applications of framing and loss aversion, Political Psychology, 25, 3:331-362.

Bohlander,G.; Snell, S. & Sherman, A. (2001). Managing Human Resources, South Western College Publishing, Cincinnati,OH.

Boisot, M. (1998). Knowledge Assets: Securing Competitive Advantage in the Information Economy, Oxford University Press, Oxford.

Boselie, P. (2014). Strategic Human Resource Management, Mcgraw-Hull, New York.

Boselie, P.; Dietz, G. & Boon, C. (2005). Commonalities and contradictions in HRM and performance research, Human Resource Management Journal, 15, 3:67-94.

Boxall, P. (1996). The strategic HRM debate and the resource based view of the firm, Human Resource Management Journal, 6, 3:59-75.

Boxall, P. F. (2007). The Goals of HRM, in Boxal, P.; Purcell, J. & Wright, P. (eds.). The Oxford Handbook of Human Resource Management, Oxford. S. 48-67.

Boxall,P.F. & Purcell, J. (2003). Strategy and Human Resource Management, Palgrave Macmillan, Basingstoke.

Boxall, P. & Purcell, J. (2008). Strategy and Human Resource Management, Palgrave, Basingstoke.

Boxall, P.F. & Purcell, J. (2010). An HRM perspective on Employee Participation, in Wilkinson, A.; Golan, P.J.; Marchington, M.& Lewins, D. (eds.). The Oxford Handbook of Participation in Organizations, Oxford University Press, Oxford, s. 129-151.

Boxall, P.F.; Purcell, J. & Wright, P. (2007). Human Resource Management: Scope, Analysis, and Significance, in Boxall, P.F.; Purcell, J. & Wright, P., The Oxford Handbook of Human Resource Management, Oxford University Press, Oxford. s. 1-16.

Boudreau, J. & Lawler, E.E. (2009). Achieving Excellence in Human Resources Management, Stanford University Press, Palo Alto.

Bowden, W. (1965). Industrial Society in England, Routledge, London.

Bowen, D.E. & Ostroff, C. (2004). Understanding HRM-firm performance linkages; the role of the strength of the HRM system, Academy of Management Review, 29, 2:203-221.

Boye, D.M. (2011). Storytelling and the Future of Organizations, Routledge, London.

Bratianu, C. (2015). Organizational knowledge dynamics, Information Science Reference, New York.

Bratton, J. & Gold, J. (2012). Human Resource Management:

Theory and Practice, Palgrave London.

Braudel, F. (1982). On history, University of Chicago Press, Chicago.

Brockbank, W. (2013). Overview and Logic, in Ulrich, D.; Brockbank, W.; Younger, J. & Ulrich, M. (eds.), Global HR Competencies: Mastering Competitive Value from the Outside in, McGraw Hill, New York. S. 3-27.

Brockbank, W. & Ulrich, D. (2006). Higher Knowledge for Higher Aspirations, Human Resource Management Journal, 44:4:489-504.

Bryant, A. (2010). The SAGE Handbook of Grounded Theory, Sage, London.

Brynjolfsson, E. & McAfee, A. (2014). The Second machine Age, W.W. Noron, New York.

Bunge, M. (1967). Scientific Research, Vol. 3, in studies of the foundations methodology and philosophy of science, Springer Verlag, Berlin.

Bunge, M. (1974). Sense and Reference, Reidel, Dordrecht.

Bunge, M. (1974a). Interpretation and Truth, Reidel, Dordrecht.

Bunge, M. (1977). Treatise on basic philosophy. Vol. 3. Ontology I: The furniture of the world. Dordrecht, Holland: D. Reidel.

Bunge, M. (1974). Sense and Reference, Reidel, Dordrecht.

Bunge, M. (1979). A World of Systems, Reidel, Dordrecht.

Bunge, M. (1981). Scientific materialism. Boston, USA: D. Reidel.

Bunge, M. (1983). Exploring the World: Epistemology & Methodology I, Dordrecht: Reidel.

Bunge, M. (1983a). Understanding the World: Epistemology & Methodology II, Dordrecht: Reidel.

Bunge, M. (1985). Philosophy of Science and Technology, Part I, Reidel, Dordrecht.

Bunge, M. (1985a). Philosophy of Science and Technology. Part II: Epistemology & Methodology. Dordrecht: Reidel.

Bunge, M. (1989). Ethics: The Good and the Right, Reidel, Dordrecht.

Bunge, M. (1989a). Treatise on basic philosophy. Vol. 8. Ethics: The good and the right. Dordrecht, Holland: D. Reidel.

Bunge, M. (1989b). Game theory is not a useful tool for the political scientist. Epistemologia, 12(1), 195–212.

Bunge, M. (1990). Boudon on anti-realism in social studies, I Weingartner,P. &

Dorn, G,J.W. Studies on Mario Bunges treatise, pp. 613-616, Rodopi, Amsterdam.

Bunge, M. (1995). The poverty of rational choice theory. In I. Jarvie & N. Laor (Eds.), Critical rationalism, metaphysics and sciences (Vol. 1, pp. 149–168). Dordrecht: Kluwer Academic Publishers.

Bunge, M. (1996). Finding philosophy in social science. New Haven: Yale University Press.

Bunge M. (1996a). The seven pillars of Popper's social philosophy, Philosophy of the social sciences, 26, 4: 528-556.

Bunge, M. (1997). Mechanism and explanation. Philosophy of the Social Sciences 27: 410- 465.

Bunge, M. (1997a). Foundations of Biophilosophy, Springer Verlag, Berlin.

Bunge, M. (1998). Philosophy of science: From problem to theory, Volume one, Transaction Publishers, New Jersey.

Bunge, M. (1998a). Philosophy of science: From explanation to Justification, Volume Two, Transaction Publishers, New Jersey.

Bunge, M. (1998b). Social science under debate: A philosophical perspective. Toronto: University of Toronto Press.

Bunge, M. (1998c). Philosophy of science: From explanation to justification, Volume two, Transaction Publishers, New Jersey.

Bunge, M. (1999). The sociology-philosophy connection. New Brunswick, NJ: Transaction.

Bunge, M. (2000). Ten modes of individualism—none of which works—and their alternatives. Philosophy of the Social Sciences, 30(3), 384–406.

Bunge, M. (2001a). Philosophy in crisis: The need for reconstruction. Amherst, NY: Prometheus Books.

Bunge, M. (2001b). Rational choice theory: A critical look at its foundations. In M. Mahner (Ed.), Scientific realism: Selected essays of Mario Bunge (pp. 303–319). Amherst, NY: Prometheus Books.

Bunge, M. (2001c). Systems and emergence, rationality and imprecision, free-wheeling and evidence, science and ideology: Social science and its philosophy according to van den Berg. Philosophy of the Social Sciences, 31(3), 404–423.

Bunge, M. (2003). Emergence and convergence: Qualitative novelty and the unity of knowledge, University of Toronto Press, Toronto.

Bunge, M. (2006a). Chasing reality: Strife over realism. Toronto: University of Toronto Press.

Bunge, M. (2006b). A systemic perspective on crime. In P.-O. H. Wikström & R. J. Sampson (Eds.), The explanation of crime: Context, mechanisms, and development (pp. 8–30). Cambridge: Cambridge University Press.

Bunge, M. (2007). Review of moral sentiments and material interests. Philosophy of the Social Sciences, 37(4), 543–547.

Bunge, M. (2009). Political philosophy: Fact, fiction and vision. New Brunswick, NJ: Transaction Publishers.

Bunge, M. (2010a). Matter and mind: A philosophical inquiry. New York: Springer.

Bunge, M. (2010b). Soziale Mechanismen und mechanismische Erkla¨rungen. Berliner Journal für Soziol- ogie, 20, 371–381.

Bunge, M. (2014). Evaluating Philosophies, Springer, Berlin.

Bunge, M., & Ardila, R. (1987). Philosophy of psychology. New York: Springer-Verlag.

Burns, T. & Stalker, G.M. (1994). The Management of Innovation, Oxford University Press, Oxford (først utgitt i 1961).

Burton-Jones, A. (1999). Knowledge Capitalism: Business, Work, and Learning in the New Economy, Oxford University Press, Oxford.

Cabrales, L.; Luno, P. & Cabrera, V. (2009). Knowledge as a mediator between HRM practices and innovative activity, Human Resource Management, 48, 4:485-503.

Cao, Q.; Simsek, Z. & Zhang, H. (2010). Modeling the joint impact of the CEO and the TM Ton organizational ambidexterity,

Journal of Management Studies, 47:1272-1296.

Campbell, D. T. (1975). Degrees of Freedom and the Case Study, Comparative Political Studies, 8, 1:178-191.

Campbell, D. T & Stanley, J. C. (1966). Experimental and Quasi-Experimental designs for research, Rand McNally, Chicago.

Carayannopoulos S. (2009). How technology-based new firms leverage newness and smallness to commercialize disruptive technologies. Entrepreneurship Theory and Practice, 33(2), 419–438.

Cardy, R.L. & Keefe, T.J. (1994). Observational purpose and evaluative articulation in frame-of-reference training: The effects of alternative processing modes on rating accuracy, Organizational Behavior and Human Decision Processes, 57:338-357.

Castelfranchi, C. (2007). Six critical remarks on science and the construction of the knowledge society. Journal of Science Communication, 6(4), 1-3.

Castells, M. (1997). The information age: Economy, society and culture, Vol II: The power of identity,

Chaklomin, V. (2015). Self-Management and Self_Marketing, CreateSpace, New York.

Chandraekaren, A.; Linderman, K. & Schraeder, R. (2012). Antecedents to Ambidexterity competency in high Technology Organizations, Journal of Operations Management, 30:134-151.

Chang, S-J. (2008). Sony vs. Samsung: The inside story of the electronic giants battle for global supremacy, John Wiley and Sons, Singapore.

Chapman, G.B. & Johnson, E.J. (2002). Incorporating the irrelevant: Anchors in judgments of belief and value, i Gilovich; Griffin & Kahneman, Heuristics and biases: The psychology of intuitive judgment, Cambridge University Press, Cambridge. S. 120-138.

Chesbrough, H.W. (2003). Open innovation: The new imperative for creating and profiting from technology, Harvard Business School press, Boston.

Chesbrough, H.W. (2006). Open business models, Harvard Business School Press, Boston. Chesbrough, H.W. (2003). Open innovation: The new imperative for creating and profiting from technology, Harvard Business School press, Boston.

Chesbrough, H.W. (2006). Open business models, Harvard Business School Press, Boston.

Chesbrough, H.; vanhavebeke, W. & West, J. (2008). Open Innovation: Researching a New Paradigm, OUP, Oxford.

Christensen, C.M. (1997). The Innovator's Dilemma: When New Technologies Cause Great Firms to Fail. Boston: Harvard Business School Press.

Clemson, B. (1984). Cybernetics: A New Management Tool, Albains Press, New York.

Combs, J.; Liu, Y.; Hall, A. & Ketchen, D. (2006). How much do high-performance work practices matter? A meta-analysis of their effects on organizational performance, Personnel Psychology, 59:501-526.

Cortada, James W. (1998). Rise of the Knowledge Worker, Butterworth-Heinemann, Boston.

Danna, K. & Griffin, R.W. (1999). Health and Well-being in the workplace: a review and synthesis of the litterature, Journal of Management, 25, 3:357-384.

Darwish, T.K. (2013). Strategic HRM and Performance: Theory and Practice, Cambridge Scolars Publishing, Cambridge.

Davenport, T. H. (2005). Thinking for a Living, How to Get Better Performance and Results from Knowledge Workers, Harvard Business School Press, Boston.

Delery, J.E. & Doty, D.H. (1996). Modes of theorizing in strategic human resource management: test of universalistic, contingency and configurational performance predictions,

Academy of Management Journal, 39, 4:802-835.

Delery, J.E. & Shaw, J. (2001). The strategic management of people in work organizations: review, synthesis and extension, Research in Personnel and Human Resources Management, 20:165-197.

Deleuze, G. & Guattari, F. (2011). What is Philosophy, Verso, London.

De Wit, B. & Meyer, R. (2014). Strategy, Process, Content, Context: An International Perspective, MPS, MacMillan, New York.

Diamond, J. (1996). The Roots of Radicalism, The New York Review of Books, 14. November, pp. 4-6.

DiMaggio, P. & Powell, W. (1983). The iron cage revisited: institutional isomorphism and collective rationality in organizational fields, American Sociological Review, 48:147-160.

Dogan, M. & Pelassy, D. (1990). How to Compare Nations: Strategies in Comparative Politics, Chatam House, Chatham.

Drucker, P.F. (1959). Landmarks of Tomorrow, Heinemann, New York.

Drucker, P.F. (1969). The age of discontinuity: Guidelines to our changing society, Harper & Row, New York.

Drucker, P.F. (1986). The changed world economy, Foreign Affairs, 64: 768-791.

Drucker, P.F. (1988). The Coming of the New Organization, Harvard Business Review, jan.feb. reprint, 88105. Pp. 1-25.

Drucker, P.F.(1993). Post-capitalist Society, Butterworth Heineman, New York.

Drucker, P. (1988). The coming of the new organization, Harvard Business Review, 88: 45-53.

Drucker, P.F. (1999). Knowledge worker productivity: The biggest challenge, California management Review, 41, 2: 79-94.

Drucker. P.F. (1999a). Management Challenges for the 21st Century. Harper Collins, New York.

Drucker, P.F. (2005). Managing oneself, Harvard Business Review, Jan: 100-109.

Duncan, R. (1976). The Ambidextrual Organization: Designing Dual Structures for Innovation, In Kilman, R.H.; Pondy, L.R. & Slevin, D. (eds.). The management of Organization, North Holland, New York. S. 167-188.

Einstein, A. (1936). Physics and Reality, J. Franklin Inst., 221:349-382

Eisenhardt, K.M. & Martin, J.A. (2000). Dynamic Capabilities:

What are they?, Strategic management Journal, 21:1105-1121.

Elster, J. (1986). Rational choice, New York University Press, New York.

Elster, J. (2010). Explaining Social Behavior: More Nuts and Bolts for the Social Sciences", Cambridge University Press, Cambridge.

Epley, N. & Gilovich, T. (2002). Putting adjustment back in the anchoring and adjustment heurustic, i Gilovich; Griffin & Kahneman, Heuristics and biases: The psychology of intuitive judgment, Cambridge University Press, Cambridge. S. 139-149.

Evans, R. (2001). The Human Side of School Change, Jossey-Bass, London.

Facklam, M. & Johnson, P. (1992). Bee Dance and Whales Sing: The Mysteries of Animal Communication, Sierra Club. New York.

Fairlough, G. (2007). Three Ways of Getting Things Done: Hierarchy, Heterarchy and Responsible Autonomy in Organizations, Triarchy Press, New York.

Feyerabend, P. (1993). Against Method, Verso, London.

Fisher, J.D. (2006). The Dynamic Effects of Neutral and Investment-Specific Technology Shocks, Journal of Political Economy, 114, 3:413-451.

Flyvbjerg, B. (2006). Five Misunderstandings about Case-Study

Research, Qualitative Inquiry, vol. 12, 2:219-245.

Forbes, P. (2005). The Gecko's Foot: How Scientists are Taking a Leaf from Nature's Book, Harper, London.

Foster, P.A. (2014). The Open Organization, Gower, New York.

Florida, R. (2008). Who's your city? Basic Books, new York.

Fombrum, C.; Tichy, N. & Devanna, A. (1984). Strategic Human Resource Management, Wiley, Hoboken, NJ.

Foss, N. J. (2009). Alternative research strategies in the knowledge movement: From macro bias to micro-foundations and multi-level explanation, European Management Review, 6:16-68.

Fox, E.; Ridgewell, A. & Ashwin, C. (2009). Looking on the bright side, Proceedings of the Royal Society B, 276:1747-1751.

Freeman, M. (1985). Free to choose, Avon Books, New York.

Fuller, A. & Unwin, L. (2004). Expansive Learning Environment: integrating personal and organizational development, in Rainbird, H.; Fuller, A. & Munro, A. Workplace Learning in Context, Routledge, London.

Galbraith, J. (1967). The New Industrial State, Houghton Mifflin, New York.

Gardner, T.M.; Wright,P.M. & Moynihan, L.M. (2011). The

impact of motivation, empowerment, and skillenhancing practices on aggregate voluntary turnover: The mediating effect of collective affective commitment, Personnel Psychology, 64:315-350.

Garud, R.; Kumaraswamy, A. &,Langlois, R. (2002). Managing in the Modular Age: New Perspectives on Architectures, Networks and Organizations, Wiley-Blackwell, New York.

Gavin, E.S. (2011). The Art and Science of the CHRO Role, in Wright, P.M. m.fl., Jossey-Bass, London. S. 23-31.

Gerhart, B. (2007). Horizontal and vertical fit in human resource systems, I Ostroff, C. & Judge, T.A. (Red.). Perspectives on Organizational fir, Psychology Press, New York. S. 317-348.

Gershuny, J. & Fisher, K. (2014). Post-industrious society: Why work time will not disappear for our grandchildren,, Center for Time Use Research, Department of Sociology, University of Oxford.

Gibson, C.B. & Birkinshaw, J. (2004). The Antecedents, Consequences and Mediating Role of Organizational Ambidexterity, Academy of Management Journal, 47:209-226.

Giddens, A. & Turner, J. (Eds.) (1987). Social Theory Today, Polity Press, Cambridge.

Griffins, L. J.; Botsko, C.; Wahl, A-M & Isaac, L.W. (1991). Theoretical Generality, Case Particularity, in Ragin, C. (Ed.)

Issues and Alternatives in Comparative Social Research, Brill, Leiden. S. 110-136.

Gilovich, T.; Griffin, D. & Kahneman, D. (2002). Heuristics and biases: The psychology of intuitive judgment, Cambridge University Press, Cambridge.

Godard, J. (1998). Workplace reforms, managerial objectives and managerial outcomes: the perceptions of Canadian IR/HRM managers, International Journal of Human Resource Management, 9, 1:18-40.

Godard, J. (2001). Beyond the high-performance paradigm? An analysis of variation in Cabadian managerial perceptions of reforme programme effectiveness, British Journal of Industrial Relations, 39, 1:25-52.

Godard, J. (2004). A critical assessment of the high-performance paradigm, British Journal of Industrial Relations, 42, 2:439-478.

Godard, J. (2010). What is best for workers?The implication of workplace and human resource management practices revisited, Industrial Relations, 49, 3:466-488.

Godard, J. & Delaney, J. (2000). Reflections on the high-performance paradigms implications for industrial relations as a field, Industrial and labor Relations Review, 53, 3:482-502.

Goleman, D. (1996). Emotional intelligence, Blumsbury

Publishing, New York.

Golman, D. (2007). Social intelligence, Arrow books, New York.

Grant, R.M. (1991). The Resource-Based Theory of Competitive Advantage: Implications for Strategy Formulation, California Management Review, 33:114-135.

Grant, R.M. (1996). Towards a knowledge based theory of the firm, Strategic Management Journal, 17:109-122.

Grant, R.M. (2000). Shifts in the world economy: The drivers of knowledge management, i Chauvel, D. & Despress, C. (Red.). Knowledge Horizons: The present and the promise of knowledge, Butterworth-Heineman, Oxford.

Grant, R.M. (2003). The Knowledge-Based View of the Firm, i Faulkner, D. & Campell, A. (red.). The Oxford Handbook of Strategy, Oxford University Press, Oxford. S. 203-231.

Grant, R.M. (2012). Contemporary Strategy Analysis, John Wiley & Sons, New York.

Grant, A. M., & Berg, J. M. (2010). Prosocial motivation at work: How making a difference makes a difference. In K. Cameron and G. Spreitzer (Red.), *Handbook of Positive Organizational Scholarship*. Oxford University Press. S. 28-44.

Grant, D. & Shields, J. (2002). In search of the subject: researching employee reactions to human resource management,

Journal of Industrial Relations, 44, 3:313-334.

Green, D.P. & Shapiro, I. (1994). Pathologies of Rational Choice: A critiqueof applications in political science, Yale University Press, New Haven, CT.

Greene, K.B. de (1982). The Adaptive Organization, John Wiley & Sons, New York.

Greenstein, S. & Devereux, M. (2006). The crisis of Encyclopedia Britannica, Kellogg School of Management, Northwestern University.

Griffin, R. & Moorhead, G. (2014). Organizational Behavior: managing People and Organizations, South Western Cengage learning, Mason, OH.

Gross, M. (2010). Ignorance and Surprise: Science, Society, and Ecological Design. Cambridge, MA: MIT Press.

Guest, D.E. (1987). Human Resource Management and Industrial Relations, Journal of Management Studies, 14, 5:503-521.

Guest, D.E. (1989a). Human Resource Management: Its Implication for industrial Relation, in Strorey, J. (Ed.). New Perspectives in Human Resource Management, Routledge, London.

Guest, D.E. (1989b). Personnel and HRM: can you tell the difference? Personnel management, january: 48-51.

Guest, D.E. (1991). Personnel Management. The End of Orthodoxy, British Journal of Industrial Relations, 29, 2:149-176.

Guest, D.E. (2007). HRM and the Worker: Towards a new Psychological Contract, in Boxall, P.; Purcell, J. & Wright, P.; The Oxford Handbook of Human Resource Management, Oxford University Press, Oxford. S. 128-146.

Guest, D. (2011). Human Resource Management and performance: still searching for some answers, Human Resource Management Journal, 21, 1:3-13.

Guthrie, J. (2000). Alternative pay practices and employee turnover: an organization economics perspective, Group & Organization Management, 25,4:419-439.

Haag, S.; Cummings, M.; McCubbrey, D.; Pinsonneault, A.; Donovan, R. (2012). Management Information Systems for the Information Age, McGraw Hill, Ryerson.

Hamel, G. (2002). Leading the Revolution: How to Thrive in Turbulent Times by Making Innovation a Way of Life, Harvard Business School Press, Boston.

Hamel, G. (2007). The furure of management, Harvard Business School Press, Boston.

Hamel, G. (2008). Introduction, i Skarzynski, P. & Gibson, R. Innovation to the core, Harvard Business Press, Boston, s. xvii-xix.

Hamel, G. (2012). What matters now: How to win in a world of relentless change Ferocious Competition, and Unstoppable Innovation, John Wiley & Sons, New York.

Hamel, G. & Prahalad, C.K. (1996). Competing for the future, Harvard Business School Press, Boston.

Han, J. (2011). Data Mining: Concepts and Techniques, Morgan Kaufman, New York.

Hannah, E.; Scott, J.; Trommer, S. (2015). Expert knowledge in Global Trade, Routledge, London.

Hansen, M. (2015). Feedforward, University of Chicago Press, Chicago.

Harman, J. (2013). The Shark´s Paintbrush: Biomicry and how Nature is Inspiring Innovation, White Cloud Press, New York.

Harris, P.R. (2005). Managing the knowledge culture, HRH Press, Amherst, MA.

Harvey, T.R. (2010). Resistance to Change, R & L Education, London.

Hedberg, B. (1997). Virtual organizations and beyond : Discover imaginary systems. New York: John Wiley & Sons.

Helfat, C.; Finkelstein, S.; Mitchel, W.; Peteraf, M.; Sing, H.; Teece, D. & Winter, S. (2007). Dynamic Capabilities, OUP, Oxford.

Henderson R. (1993). Underinvestment and incompetence as responses to radical innovation: Evidence from the photolithographic alignment equipment industry. RAND Journal of Economics, 24(2), 248-270.

Hewing, M. (2013). Collaboration with potential users for discontinuous innovation, Springer Gabler, Potsdam.

Hirst, P. (1993). Globalization is fashionable but is it a myth? Guardian, 22 mars.

Hlupic, W. (2014). The management Shift, Palgrave Macmillian, New York.

Homans, G.C. 81964). Bringing Men back in, American Sociological Review, 29:809-818.

Hsieh, C-T. & Kienow, P. (2007). Relative Prices and Relative Prosperity, The American Economic Review, 97, 3:562-585.

Huber, G.P. (1984). The Nature and Design of Post-Industrial Organizations, Management Science,30, 8:928-951.

Huber, G.P. (1991). Organizational Learning: The Contributing Processes and Literatures, Organization Science, 2:88-115.

Huselid, M.A (1995). The impact of human resource management practices on turnover productivity, and corporate performance, Academy of Management Journal, 38, 3:635-672.

Hutton, W. (1995). Myth that sets the world to right, Guardian, 12 june, s. 17.

Innerarity, D. (2012). Power and knowledge: The politics of the knowledge society, European Journal of Social Theory, 16(1), 3-16.

Jackson, S.E.; Schuler, R.S. & Rivero, J. (1989). Organizational characteristics as predictors of personnel practices, Personnel Psychology, 42:727-786.

Jansen, J.J.P.; Van den Borch, F.A.J. & Volberda, H.W.C. (2006). Exploratory innovation, Exploitative innovation, and Performance: Effects of Organizational antecedents and environmental moderators, Management Science, 52: 1661-1674.

Jemielniak, D. (2012). The New Knowledge Workers, Edward Elgar, Cheltenham.

Jiang, K.; Lepak, D.P.; Hu, J. & Baer, J.C. (2012). How does Human Resource Management Influence Organizational Outcomes? A Meta-Analytic Investigation of Mediating Mechanisms, Academy of Management Journal, 55, 6:1264-1294.

Johannessen, J-A. & Olaisen, J. (1993). The information intensive organization: A study

of governance, control and communication in a Norwegian shipyard; International Journal of

Information Management, Vol. 13, 5:341-354.

Johannessen, J-A. & Hauan, A. (1994). Organizational Cybernetics: The Ecology of Change in a Norwegian Shipyard, Kybernetes, 23, 8:11-26.

Johannessen, J-A.; Hauan, A. & Olaisen, J. (1996). Strategies for Innovation, A

Longitudinal Case Study Approach, Fagbokforlaget, Oslo (ISBN:82-7674-227-0).

Johannessen, J-A.; Olaisen, J. & Olsen, B. (2001). Mismanagement of tacit knowledge:

the importance of tacit knowledge, the danger of information technology, and what to do

about it? International Journal of Information Management, 21, 3:3-20.

Johannessen, J-A.; Olsen, B. & Lumpkin, G.T. (2001). Innovation as newness: What is new, how new, and new to whom? European Journal of Innovation Management, 4, 1:20-31.

Johannessen, J.-A. & J. Olaisen (2005). Systemic philosophy and the philosophy of social science-Part I: Transcendence of the naturalistic and the anti-naturalistic position in the philosophy of social science, Kybernetes Vol 34 No 7/8, 1261-1277.

Johannessen, J.-A. & J. Olaisen (2006). Systemic philosophy and the philosophy of social science-Part II: The systemic position, Kybernetes Vol 34 No 9/10, 1570-1586.

Johannessen, J.-A. & J. Olaisen (2006a). Hva er vitenskap? (What is Science?) Fagbokforlaget, Oslo.

Johannessen, J-A., Olaisen, J. & Olsen. B. (2001). Mismanagement of Tacit Knowledge: The Importance of Tacit Knowledge, the Danger of Information Technology, and What to do about it? International Journal of Information Technology, 21, 1:3-20.

Jones, G. (1984). Task visibility, free riding, and shirking: Explaining the effect of structure

and technology on employee behavior, Academy of Management Review, 9:684-695.

Kahneman, D. (2011). Thinking fast and slow, Allen Lane, New York.

Kahneman, D. & Frederick, S. (2002). Representativeness revisited: Attribute substitution in intuitive judgment, i Gilovich, T.; Griffin, D. & Kahneman, D. Heuristics and biases: The psychology of intuitive judgment, Cambridge University Press, Cambridge. S. 49-81.

Kahneman, D. & Tversky, A. (1979). An analysis of decision under risk, Econometrica, Journal of the econometric society,

47,2:263-292.

Kahneman, D. & Tversky, A. (2000). Prospect Theory: An analysis of decision under risk, i Kahneman, D. & Tversky, A. (Red.). Choices, values and frames, Cambridge University Press, Cambridge. S. 17-43.

Kahneman, D. & Tversky, A. (2000). Prospect Theory: An analysis of decision under risk, i Kahneman, D. & Tversky, A. (Red.). Choices, values and frames, Cambridge University Press, Cambridge. S. 17-43.

Kahneman, D.; Slovic, P. & Tversky, A. (1982). Judgment under uncertainty: Heuristics and biases, Cambridge University Press, Cambridge.

Karabarbounis, L. & Neiman, B. (2013). The Global Decline of the Labor Share, NBER Working Chapter nr. 19136.

Kehoe, R.R. & Wright, P.M. (2013). The impact of high performance human resource practices on employees attitudes and behaviors, Journal of Management,39, 2:366-391.

Kirzner, S. (1982). The theory of entrepreneurship in economic growth; in Kent, C.A.; Sexton, D. L. & Vesper, K.H. (Ed.). Encyclopedia of Entrepreneurship, Prentice Hall, Englewood Cliffs. N.J.

Kuhn, T. (2012). The Structure of Scientific Revolutions,

University of Chicago Press, Chicago.

Kuran, T. & Sunstein, C.R. (1999). Availabilities cascades and risk regulation, Stanford Law Review, 51: 683-768.

Kuznet, S. (1940). Schumpeter´s Business Cycles, American Economic Review, 257-271.

Lakhtakia, A. (2013). Engineered Biomimicry, Elsevier, London.

Latham, G.; Sulsky, L.M. & MacDonald, H. (2007). Performance Management, i Boxall, P.; Purcell, J. & Wright, P. (red.). The Oxfoed Handbook of Human Resource Management, Oxford University Press, Oxford. S. 364-381.

Le Deist, F.D. & Winterton, J. (2005). What is competence? Human Resource Development International, 8, 1:27-46.

Lee, A.S. (1989). Case Studies as Natural Experiments, Human Relations, 42, 2: 117-137.

Lele, C.G. (2011). Organizational Democracy: Collaborative Team Culture: Key to

Organizational Growth, Atlantic Publisher, New York.

Leontief, W. (1966). Input-Output Economics, Oxford University Press, Oxford.

Legge, K. (1978). Power, Innovation and Problem Solving in Personnel Management, McGraw-Hill, Maidenhead.

Legge, K. (1989). Human Resource Management: A Critical Analysis, in Storey, J. (Ed). New Perspectives in Human Resource Management, Routledge, London. S. 19-40.

Legge, K. (2005). Human Resource Management: Rhetorics and Realities, Macmillan, Basingstoke.

Leistner, F. (2010). Mastering organizational knowledge flow, John Wiley & Sons, New York.

Lengnick-Hall, M.L. & Lengnick-Hall, C.A. (2003). Human Resource Management in the Knowledge Economy, BK, San Francisco.

Lepak, D. & Snell, S. (1999). The strategic management of human capital:determinants and implications of different relationnships, Academy of management Review, 24, 1:1-18.

Lepak, D.P.; Liao, H.; Chung, Y. & Harden, E. (2006). A conceptual review of HR management systems in strategic HRM research, Research in Personnel and Human Resource Management, 25:217-272.

Liao,H.; Toya, K.; Lepak, D.P. & Hong, Y. (2009). Do they see eye to eye? Management and employee perspective og high-performance work systems and influence processes on service quality, Journal of Applied Psychology, 94:371-391.

Liker, J. (2004). The Toyota way, Mcgraw-Hill, New York.

Liker, J. (2011). The Toyota Way to Lean Leadership: Achieving and Sustaining Excellence through Leadership Development, McGraw-Hill, New York.

Liker, J. & Convis, G.L. (2014). The Toyota way to Lean Leadership, Mc.Graw-Hill, New York.

Luhmann, N. (1989). Ecological Communication, Polity Press, Cambridge.

Luhmann, N. (1995). Social Systems, Stanford University Press, Stanford.

Luthans, F.; Youssef-Morgan, C.M. & Avolio, B.J. (2015). Psychological Capital and Beyond, OUP, New York.

Luttwak, E. (1999). Turbo capitalism, Harper, New York.

Mabey, C.; Salaman, G. & Storey, J. (2002). Strategic Human Rseource Management: The Theory of Practice and the Practice of Theory, I Mabey, C. Salaman, G. & Storey, J. (Red.). Strategic Human Resource Management, Sage, London. S. 1-13.

Maciariello, J.A. (2014). A Year With Peter Drucker, Harper Business, New York.

Maciariello, J.A & Linkletter, K.E. (2011). Druckers lost art of management, McGraw-Hill, New York.

Machlup, F. (1962). The production and distribution of knowledge in the United States, Princeton University Press, princeton, NJJ.

Machlup, F. (1981). Knowledge and knowledge production, Princeton University press, Princeton.

Machlup, F. & Kronwinkler, T. (1975). Workers who produce knowledge: A steady increase 1900 to 1970, Weltwirtschaftliches Archiv, 3: 752-759.

Mahoney, T. & Deckop, J. (1986). Evolution of Concept and Practice in Personel Administration/Human Resource Management, Journal of Management, 12:223-241.

Mahoney, J.T. & Pandian, J.R. (1992). The resource-based view within the conversation of strategic management, Strategic Management Journal, 13:363-380.

Maier, J. (2015). The Ambidextrous Organization: Exploring the New While Exploiting the Now, Palgrave Macmillan, New York.

Malkiel, B.G. (2012). A Random Walk Down Wall Street: The Time-Tested Strategy for Successful Investing, W.W. Norton, New York.

Mandel, D.R. (2001). Gain-loss framing and choice: Separating outcome formulations from desciptor formulations, Organizational Behavior and Human Descision Processes, 85, 1:56-76.

March, J.G. (1991). Exploration and Exploitation in Organizational Learning, Organizational Science, 2:71-87.

Marr, A. (1995). The real enemy is the moneymarket, Spectator, 9.sept. s. 20-21.

Mathis, R. & Jackson, J.H. (2008). Human Resource Management, South Western Cengage Learning, Cincinati, OH.

Maurer, K. (2012). The spirit of kaizen, McGraw-Hill, New York.

May, T.Y.; Korczynski, M. & Frenkel, S.J. (2002). Organizational and Occupational Commitment: Knowledge workers in Large Organizations, Journal of Management Studies, 39, 6:775-801.

McCarthy, I.P. & Gordon,B.R. (2011). Schieving Contextual Ambidexterity in R&D Organizations: A Management Control System Approach, R&D Management, 41:240-258.

Mcdermott, M. (2005). Knowledge Workers: You can gauge their effectiveness, Leadership Excellence 22 (10): 15–17.

McDermott, R. (2001). Risk-taking in international politics: Prospect theory in American foreign policy, The University of Mitchigan Press, Michigan.

Mcdermott, M. (2005). Knowledge Workers: You can gauge their effectiveness, Leadership Excellence 22 (10): 15–17.

Mello, J.A. (2006). Strategic Management of Human Resources, South Western Learning, Cincinati, OH.

Merton, R.K. (1957). The Role Set: Problems in Sociological Theory, British Journal of Sociology, 8:106-120.

Messersmith, J.; Patel, P.; Lepak, D. & Gold-Williams, J.S. (2011). Unlocking the black box: exploring the link between high-performance work systems and performance, Journal of Applied Psychology, 99, 6:1105-1118.

Michaels, E.; Hanfield-Jones, H. & Axelrod, B. (2001). The War for Talent, Harvard Business School Press, Boston.

Miller, J.G. (1978). Living Systems, McGraw-Hill, New York.

Minbaeva, D.B. (2008). HRM practices affecting extrinsic and intrinsic motivation of knowledge receivers and their effect on intra-MNC knowledge transfer, International Business Review, 17, 6:703-713.

Minbaeva, D.B.; Foss, N. & Snell, S. (2009). Guest editors introduction: Bringing the knowledge Perspective into HRM, Human Resource Management, 48, 4:477-483.

Minbaeva, D.B. (2013). Strategic HRM in building micro-foundations of organizational knowledge-based performance, Human Resource Management Review, 23:378-390.

Minzberg, H. (1997). The nature of managerial work, Prentice Hall, New York.

Mongkhonvanit, M.J. (2010). Industrial Cluster and Higher

Education, Xlibris, London.

Morgan, G. (1988). Holographic Organization and the New Technology, Unpublished Chapter York University, Toronto.

Morgan, G. (1989). Organisasjonsbilder, Universitetsforlaget, Oslo.

Morgan, G. (1989a). Organisasjoner i bevegelse, Universitetsforlaget, Oslo.

Morgan, G. (2006). Images of Organizations, Sage, London.

Mosco, V.; McKercher, C. (2007). Introduction: Theorizing Knowledge Labor and the Information Society. Knowledge Workers in the Information Society., Lexington Books, Lanham.

Mowday, R. (1985). Strategies for adapting to high rates og employee turnover,uman Resource Management, 23:365-380.

Nadler, D. & Tushman, M.J. (1997). Competing by Design, The Power of Organizational Architecture, Oxford University Press, Oxford..

Negoita, C.V. (1981). Fuzzy Systems, Albacus Press, Kent.

Nelson, R,R. & Winter, S.G. (1982). An Evolutionary Theory of Economic Change, Harvard University Press, Cambridge, MA.

Nonaka, I. (1994). A Dynamic Theory of Organizational Knowledge Creation, Organization Science, 5:14-37.

Nonaka, I. & Takeuchi, H. (1995). The Knowledge Creating Company, Oxford

University Press, Oxford.

Nonaka, L. & Takeuchi, H. (2002). The Knowledge Creating Company, i Mabey, C. Salaman, G. & Storey, J. (Red.). Strategic Human Resource Management, Sage, London. S. 312-324.

Nordhaug, O. (1994). Human capital in organizations: Competence, training and learning, Scandinavian University Press, Oslo.

North, D.C. (1990). Institutions, Institutional Change and economic performance, Cambrifge University Press, Cambridge.

North, D. (1993). Nobelforedraget: http://www.nobelprize.org/nobel_prizes/economics/laureates/1993/north-lecture.html#not2, lesedato, 4.5.2012.

North, D.C. (1994). Economic performance through time, American Economic Review, 84: 359-368.

North, D.C. (1996). Epilogue: Economic performance through time. In Alston, L.J.; Eggertson, T. & North, D.C. "Empirical studies in institutional change", Cambridge University Press, Cambridge (pp.342-355).

North, D.C. (1997). Prologue, 3-13 in J.N. Drobak & J.V.C. The frontiers of the new institutional economics, Academic Press, New

York.

Northcraft, G.B. & Neale, M.A. (1987). Experts, amateurs, and real estate: An anchoring- and- adjustment perspective on property pricing decisions, Organizational Behavior and Human Decision Processes, 39:84-97.

O'Connor G.C., De MartinoR. (2006). Organizing for radical innovation: an exploratory study of the structural aspects of RI management systems in large established firms. Journal of Product Innovation Management. Journal of Product Innovation Management, 23(6), 475–497.

OECD (2000*a*), *A New Economy? The changing role of innovation and information technology in growth,* Paris.

OECD (2000*b*), *Economic Outlook,* Paris.

OECD (2000*c*), *Education at a Glance: OECD Indicators,* CERI, Paris.

OECD (2000*d*), "ICT Skills and Employment, Working party on the information economy", Paris, 15 November, DSTI/ICCP/IE (2000)7.

OECD (2000*e*), *Knowledge Management in the Learning Society,* CERI, Paris.

OECD (2001). Innovative clusters: Driving of national

innovation-systems, OECD, Paris.

Oliver, C. (1997). Sustainable competitive advantage: combining institutional and resource-based views, Strategic Management Journal, 18, 9:697-713.

O'Reilly, C.A. & Tushman, M.L. (2004). The Ambidextrous Organization, Harvard Business Review, 82, 4:74-81.

O'Reilly, C.A. & Tushman, M.L. (2007). Ambidexterity as a dynamic capability: Resolving the innovators dilemma, Harvard Business School Press, Boston.

O'Reilly, C.A. & Tushman, M.L. (2011). Organizational Ambidexterity in Action: How managers explore and emploit, California Management Review, 53, 4:5-22.

Paauwe, J. (2004). HRM and performance: Achieving long term viability, Oxford University Press, Oxford.

Paauwe, J. (2009). HRM and performance:achievements, methodological issues and prospects, Journal of Management Studies, 46, 1:129-142.

Paauwe, J. & Boselie, P (2003). Challenging Strategic HRM and the relevance of the institutional setting, Human Resource Management Journal, 13, 3:56-70.

Paauwe, J.; Guest, D.E. & Wright, P.M. (2013). HRM & Performance: Achievements & Challenges, Wiley, London.

Paauwe, J.; Guest, D.E. & Wright, P.M. (2013a). HRM and Performance: What do we know and where should we go?, I Paauwe, J.; Guest, D.E. & Wright, P.M. (2013). HRM & Performance: Achievements & Challenges, Wiley, London. S. 1-13.

Parson, T. (1951). The Social System, Free Press, Glencoe.

Pattanayan, B. (2005). Human Resource Management, Prentice-Hall, New York.

Paauwe, J. (2004). HRM and performance: Achieving long term viability, Oxford University Press, Oxford.

Paauwe, J. (2009). HRM and performance:achievements, methodological issues and prospects, Journal of Management Studies, 46, 1:129-142.

Paauwe, J. & Boselie, P (2003). Challenging Strategic HRM and the relevance of the institutional setting, Human Resource Management Journal, 13, 3:56-70.

Paauwe, J.; Guest, D.E. & Wright, P.M. (2013). HRM & Performance: Achievements & Challenges, Wiley, London.

Paauwe, J.; Guest, D.E. & Wright, P.M. (2013a). HRM and Performance: What do we know and where should we go?, I Paauwe, J.; Guest, D.E. & Wright, P.M. (2013). HRM & Performance: Achievements & Challenges, Wiley, London. S. 1-13.

Pfeffer,J. & Sutton, R.J. (1999). Knowing what to do is not enough: Turning knowledge into action, California management Review, Vol. 42,1: 83-108.

Polanyi, M. (1962). Personal Knowledge, Routledge & Uegan Paul, London.

Polanyi, M. (1966). Tacit Knowledge, Anchor Day, New York.

Polanyi, M. (2009). The Tacit Dimension, University of Chicago Press, Chicago.

Pollatsek, A. & Tversky, A. (1970). A Theory of risk, Journal of Mathematical Psychology, 7.

Popper, K. (1959). The Logic of Scientific Discovery, Basic Books, New York.

Popper, K. (1963). Conjectures and Refutations, Routledge, London.

Porter, M. (1980). Competitive strategy. Techniques for analyzing industries and competitors, Free Press, New York.

Porter, M. (1998). Clusters and the New Economics of Competition, Harvard Business Review, nov.-dec. Pp. 77-90.

Porter, M. (2004). Competitive Strategy, Free Press, New York.

Prahalad, C. K. & Krishnan, M.S. (2008). The New Age of Innovation: Driving Cocreated Value Through Global Networks, McGraw-Hill, New York.

Priem, R. & Butler, J. (2001). Is the resource-based view a useful perspective for strategic management research? Academy of Management Review, 26, 1:22-40.

Pyöriä, P. (2005). The Concept of Knowledge Work Revisited. *Journal of Knowledge Management* 9 (3): 116–127.

Raisch, S. & Hotz, F. (2010). Shaping the Context for learning: Corporate Alignments Initiatives, Environmental Munifience and Firm Performance, I Wall, S,, Zimmerman, C., Klingebiel, R. & Lange, D. (eds.). Strategic Reconfigurations: Building Dynamic Capabilities in Rapid Innovation Based Industries, Edward Elgar, Cheltenham. S. 62-85.

Ragin, C. & Becker, H.S. (Eds.) (1992). What is a Case? Exploring the Foundations of Social Inquiry, Cambridge University Press, Cambridge.

Ramaswamy, V. & Ozcan, K. (2014). The Co-Creation Paradigm, Stanford University Press, Stanford.

Ramirez, Y.W. & Nembhard, D.A. (2004). Measuring Knowledge worker productivity, Journal of Intellectual Capital, 5, 4:602-628.

Rees, G. & Smith, P.E. (2014). Strategic Human Resource Management: An International Perspective, Sage, London.

Reich, R. (1991). The Work of Nations: Preparing ourselves for the 21st century capitalism, Simon and Schuster, London.

Reinhardt, W., Smith, B.; Sloep, P.Drachler, H. (2011). Knowledge Worker Roles and Actions – Results of Two Empirical Studies, Knowledge and Process Management 18 (3): 150–174.

Reinmoell, S. & Reinmoeller, P. (2015). The Ambidextrous Organization, Routledge, Oxford.

Rhee, Y.P. (1982). The Breakdown of Authority Structure in Korea in 1960: A Systems Approach, Seoul National University Press, Seoul.

Rios, J.P. (2012). Design and Diagnoses for Sustainable Organizations, Springer, London.

Rios-Rull, J-V. & Santaeulalia-Llopis,R. (2010). Redistributive Shocks and Productivity Shocks, Journal of Monetary Economics, 57:931-948.

Roberts, L.M.; Spreitzer, G.; Dutton, J.; Quinn, R.; Heaphy, E. &

Barker, B. (2005). How to play to your strengths, Harvard Business Review, Jan.: 74-82.

Robertson, B.J. (2015). Holocracy: The Revolutionary Management System that Abolishes Hierarchy, Penguin, London.

Rogers, E.M (2003). The Diffusion of Innovation, Simon & Schuster, New York.

Rooney, D.; Heam, G. & Kastelle, T. (2008). Handbook of the Knowledge economy, Edward Elgar, New York.

Rosing, K.; Frese, M. & Bausch, A. (2011). Explaining the heterogenity of the leadership-innovation relationship: Ambidextrous leadership, The Leadership Quarterly, 22:956-974.

Rostow, W.W. (1988). Review of Alfred Kleinknecht, Innovation Patterns in Crises, Journal of Economic Litterature, 26:111-113.

Rynes, S. (2007). Editor's Foreword: Tackling the "Great Divide" between Research Production and dissemination in Human Resource Management, Academy of Management Journal, 50: 985-986.

Sanou, B. (2013). The world in 2013: ICT fact and figures. Retrieved from http://www.itu.int/en/ITUD/Statistics/Documents/facts/ICTFactsFigures2013.pdf

Santos, D.Y. & Williamson, P. (2001). From Global to

Metanational: How Companies Win in the Knowledge Economy, Harvard Business School Press, Boston.

Sartain, L. (2001). The Future of HR, Society for Human Resource Management, Alexandria, VA.

Sassen, S. (2002). Global networks/linked cities, Routledge, New York.

Savage, C. (1995). Fifth Generation Management: Co-creating through Virtual Enterprising, Dynamic Teaming and Knowledge Networking, Butterworth-Heinemann, Boston.

Scarbrough, H. (1999). Knowledge as work: Conflicts in management of knowledge workers, Technology Analysis and Strategic management 11,1:5-16.

Schneider, B. (1987). The People Make the Place, Personnel Psychology, 40, 3:437-453.

Schneider C., Veugelers R. (2010). On young highly innovative companies: why they matter and how (not) to policy support them. Industrial and Corporate Changes, 19(4), 19 (4): 969-1007.

Schuler, R.S. & Jackson, S.E. (1987). Linking competitive strategies with human resource management practices, Academy of management Executive, 1:207-219.

Schuler, R.S. & Jackson, S.E. (2005). A quarter century review of human resource management in the US.: the growth in importance of the international perspective, Management Revue, 16,1:11-35.

Scott,W.R. (1987). The adolscence of institutional theory, Administrative Science Quarterly, 32:493-511.

Scott, W.R. (2013). Institutions and organizations: Ideas, Interest and Identities, Sage, London.

Schwaniger, M. (2008). Intelligent Organizations: Powerful Models for Systemic management, Springer, London.

Seligman, M.E.P. (2006). Learned optimism, Vintage Books, New York.

Senge, P. (1990). The Fifth Discipline: The Art and Practice of the Learning Organization, Century Business, London.

Sennett, R. (1998). The Corrosion of Character: Personal Consequences of Work in the New Capitalism, W.W. Norton & Company, New York.

Sennet, R. (2004). Respect, Norton, New York.

Sennet, R. (2006). The Culture of the New Capitalism, Yale University Press, London.

Sennett, R. (2013). The Rituals, Pleasures and Politics of

Cooperation, Penguin, London.

Seirafi, K. (2015). Organizational epistemology: Understanding knowledge in organization, Physica, New York.

Shapiro, C. & Varian, H.R. (1999). Information rules: A strategic guide to the network economy, Harvard Business School press, Boston, Mass.

Stacey, R.D. (1996). Complexity and Creativity in Organizations, Berrett-Koehler, London.

Sirmon, D., Hitt, M. & Irelanf, R. (2007). Managing firm resources in dynamic environments to create value: looking inside the black box, Academy of Management Review, 32, 1:273-292.

Skarzynski, P. & Gibson, R. (2008). Innovation to the core, Harvard Business School Press, Boston.

Smith, K.G.; Collins, C.J. & Clark, K.D. (2005). Existing Knowledge, knowledge creation capability, and the rate of new product introduction in high-technology firms, Academy of Management Journal, 48, 2:346-357.

Snowdon, D. (2001). Aging with grace: What the nun study teaches us about leading longer, healthier, and more meaningful lives, Bantam Books, New York.

Spreitzer, G.; Sutcliffe, K.; Dutton, J.; Sonenshein, S. & Grant, A.M. (2005). A Socially embedded model of thriving at work, Organization Science, 16:537-549.

Stacey, R.D. (1996). Complexity and Creativity in Organizations, Berrett-Koehler, London.

Stanford, M. (2013). Organization design: Engaging with change, Routledge, Oxford.

Stake, R. (1995). The Art of Case Study Research, Sage, Thousand Oaks.

Stalk, G.; Evans, P. & Shulman, L.E. (1993). Competing on Capabilities: the new rules of corporate strategy, I Howard, R. (Red.). The Learning Imperative: managing People for Continous Innovation, Harvard University Press, Cambridge, MA.

Steinbock, D. (2010). Winning across global markets: How Nokia creates strategic advantage in a fast changing world, Jossey-Bass, San Francisco.

Stewart, T. (1996). Taking on the last bureaucracy, Fortune, january, no. 15, 113, 1:105-107

Stigliz, J.E. & Greenwald, B.C. (2015). Creating a learning society, Columbia University Press, New York.

Storey, J. (1989). From Personnel management to Human

Resource Management, in New Perspectives in Storey, J. (Ed.). Human Resource Management, Routledge, London.

Storey, J. (1992). Development in the Management of Human Resources, Blackwell, Oxford.

Storey, J. (2001). Human Resource Management Today: An Assesment, in Storey, J. (Ed.). Human Resource Management: A Critical Text, Thompson Learning, London. S. 3-20.

Storey, J.; Ulrich, D. & Wright, P.M. (2009). Introduction, i Storey, J.; Wright, P.M. &

Ulrich, D. (red.). The Routledge Companion to Strategic Human Resource Management,

Routledge, London. S. 3-15.

Schuler, R.S. (1992). Strategic HRM: Linking People with the Need of the Business, Organizational Dynamics, 21:19-32.

Swart, J. (2007). HRM and Knowledge Workers, i Boxall, P.; Purcell, J. & Wright, P. The Oxford Handbook of Human Resource Management, Oxford University Press, Oxford. S. 450-468.

Switzer, F. & Sniezek, J.A. (1991). Judgment processes in motivation: Anchoring and adjustment effects on judgment and behavior, Organizational Behavior and Human Decision Processes, 49:208-229.

Tackeuchi, R.; Chen, R. & Lepak, D.P. (2009). Through the looking glass of social system: Cross leve effects of high-performance work systems on employees attitudes, Personnel Psychology, 62:1-29.

Tackeuchi, R.; Lepak, D.P.; Wang, H. & Takeuchi, K. (2007). An empirical examinationof the mechanisms mediating between high-performance work systems and the performance of Japanese organizations, Journal of Applied Psychology, 92:1069-1083.

Tan, P-N.; Steinbach, M., Kumar, V. (2013). Introduction to Data Mining, Pearson, New York.

Tazzi, F. (2014). Biomimicry in Organizations: Drawing inspiration from nature to find new efficient, effective and sustainable ways of managing business, Create Space, new York.

Tapscott, D. & Williams, A.D. (2006). Wikinomics: How Mass Collaboration Changes Everything, Penguin, New York.

Teece, D.J. (2011). Dynamic Capabilities and Strategic management: Organizing for

Innovation, OUP, Oxford.

Teece, D.J. (2013). Dynamic Capabilities and Strategic management: Organizing for

Innovation, OUP, Oxford.

Teece, D.; Pisano; G. & Shuen, A. (1997). Dynamic capabilities and strategic management, Strategic Management Journal, 18, 7:509-533.

Teece, D.; Pierce, J.L. & Boerner, C.S. (2002). Dynamic Capabilities, Competence, and Behavioral Theory of the firm, I Augier, M. & March, J.G. (Red.). The Economics of Change, Choice and Structure: Essays in the memory of Richart M. Cyert, Edward Elgar,Cheltenham.

Tetlock, P. (2006). Expert political judgment: How good is it?How can we know?, Princeton University Press, Princeton.

Thota, H. & Munir, Z. (2011). Key Concepts in Innovation, Palgrave Macmillan, London.

Thurow, L. (1999). Creating wealth, Nicolas Brealey, London.

Tilly, C. (1998). Durable Inequality, University of California Press, Berkeley.

Torrington, D.; Hall, L. & Taylor, S. (2014). Human Resource Management, 9. Edition, Pearson, New York.

Trompernaars, F. (2007). Riding the whirwind, The Infinited Ideas Company, Oxford.

Truss, C.; Mankin, D. & Kelliher, C. (2012). Strategic Human Resource Management, Oxford University Press, Oxford.

Tushman, M.L. & O'Reilly, C.A. (1996). Ambidextrous Organization: Managing Evolutionary and Revolutionary Change, California Management Review, 38, 4:8-30.

Tversky, A. (1972). Elimination by aspects: A theory of choice, Psychological Review, 79: 281-299.

Tversky, A. & Kahneman, D. (1974). Judgment under uncertainty: Heuristics and biases, Science, 185:1124-1131.

Tversky, A. & Kahneman, D. (1981). The framing of decisions and the psychology of choice, Science, 211: 453-458.

Tversky, A. & Kahneman, D. (1983). Extensional versus intuitive reasoning. The conjunction fallacy in probability judgment, Psychological Review, 90: 293-315.

Tversky, A. & Kahneman, D. (2000). Loss aversion in riskless choice, i Kahneman, D. & Tversky, A. (Red.). Choices, values and frames, Cambridge University Press, Cambridge. S.143-158.

Turner, J. (1987). Analytical Theorizing, in Giddens, A & Turner, J. (eds.). Social Theory Today, Polity Press, Cambridge. S. 156-195.

Turner, J. (1988). A Theory of Social Interaction, Stanford

University Press, Stanford.

Turner, J. (2002). Face to Face, Stanford University Press, Stanford.

Turner, J. (2007). Human Emotions, Routledge, London.

Turner, J. (2013). Human Institutions, Rowman & Littlefield, New York.

Ulrich, D. (1991). Using human resources for competitive advantage, I Kilman, R.; Kilman,

I. & Associates (Red.). Making Organizations Competitive, Jossey-Bass, San Francisco. S.

129-155.

Ulrich, D. (1997). Human Resource Champions, Harvard Business School Press, Boston.

Ulrich, D. (2013). Forword, in Ulrich, D.; Brockbank, W.; Younger, J. & Ulrich, M. (eds.), Global HR Competencies: Mastering Competitive Value from the Outside in, McGraw Hill, New York. S. v-xxi.

Ulrich, D. (2013a). Future of Global HR: What's Next?, in Ulrich, D.; Brockbank, W.; Younger, J. & Ulrich, M. (eds.), Global HR Competencies: Mastering Competitive Value from the Outside in, McGraw Hill, New York. S. 255-268.

Ulrich, D. & Brockbank, W. (2005). The HR Value Proposition, Harvard Business School Press, Boston, MA.

Ulrich, D. & Smallwood, N. (2006). Leadership Brand, Harvard Business School Press, Boston.

Ulrich, D. & Smallwood, N. (2007). Leadership Code, Harvard Business School Press, Boston.

Ulrich, D.; Brockbank, W.; Johnson,D.; Sandholz, K. & Younger, J. (2008). HR Competencies: Mastery at the Intersection of People and Business, RBL Group, New York.

Ulrich, D., Smallwood, N. & Sweetman, K. (2008a). The Leadership Code: Five Rules to Lead By, Harvard Business Review Press, Boston.

Ulrich, D.; Younger, J.; Brockbank, W. & Ulrich, M. (2012). HR from the Outside in: Six Compeencies for the Future of Human Resources, mcgraw Hill, New York.

Ulrich, D.; Brockbank, W.; Younger, J. & Ulrich, M. (eds.) (2013). Global HR Competencies: Mastering Competitive Value from the Outside in, McGraw Hill, New York.

Ulrich, D. & Ulrich, W. (2010). The Why of Work, McGraw Hill, New York.

UNESCO (2005). United Nations Educational, Scientific and Cultural Organization (2005). Toward knowledge societies.

UNESCO World Report. Conde-sur-Noireau, France: Imprimerie Corlet.

Urry, J. (2004). Mobile sociology, i Webster, F. The information society reader, Routledge, London, s. 190-203.

Vallima, J. & Hoffman, D. (2008). Knowledge society discourse and higher education. Higher Education, 56(3), 265-285.

Van der Lans, R.F. (2012). Business Intelligence Systems, Elsevier, New York.

Vis, B. (2010). Politics of risk-taking, Amsterdam University Press, Amsterdam.

Von Hippell, E. (2005). Democrating innovation, MIT Press, Cambridge.

Wagner, S.H. & Goffin, R.D. (1997). Difference in accuracy of absolute and comparative performance appraisal methods, Organizational Bahavior and Human Decision Processes, 70:95-103.

Walton, J. (1992). Making the Theoretical Case, in Ragin, C. & Becker, H. S. (eds.). What is a Case? Exploring the Foundations of Social Inquiry, Cambridge University Press. S. 121-137.

Wang, Q-G.; Lee, T.H. & Lin, C. (2003). Relay Feedback: Analysis, identification and control, Springer, London.

Wakker, P.P. (2010). Prospect Theory for risk and ambiguity, Cambridge University Press, Cambridge.

Walker, J. (1980). Human Resource Planning, McGraw-Hill, New York.

Walton, R.E. (1985). From Control to Commitment in the workplace, Harvard Business Review, March-April, s. 77-84.

Wang, S. & Noe, R. (2010). Knowledge sharing. A review and direction for future research, Human Resource Management Review, 20:115-131.

Warr, P. (2007). Work Happiness, and Unhappiness, Lawrence Erlbaum, London.

Webster, F. (2002). Theories of the information society, Routledge, London.

Wegge, J; Jeppesen, H.J.; Weber, G.W.; Pearce, C.L.; Silva, S.A.; Pundt, A.; Jonsson, T.;

Wilson, B. (1987). Single-case Experimental Designs in Neuro-Psychological Rehabilitation, Journal of Clinical and Experimental Neuropsychology, 9, 5:527-544.

Witten, I.H.; Frank, E. & Hall, M. (2011). Data Mining, Morgan Kaufmann, New York.

Wolf, S.; Wassenaar, C.L.; Unterrainer, C. & Piecha, A. (2010). Promoting Work Motivation in Organizations: Should Employee Involvement in Organizational Leadership Become a New Tool in the Organizational Psychologist's Kit?Journal of Personnel Psychology, 2010, vol. 9, 4:154-171, Special Issue: Shared Leadership.

Welbourne, T.M. & Cyr, L.A. (1999). The Human reource executive effect in initial public offering firms, Academy of Management Journal, 42, 6:612-629.

Welch, J. (2005). Winning, Harper Business, New York.

Wernerfelt, B. (1984). (1984). A resource-based view of the firm, Strategic Management Journal, 5, 2:171-180.

White, J. & Younger, J. (2013). The Global Perspective, in Ulrich, D.; Brockbank, W.; Younger, J. & Ulrich, M. (eds.); Global HR Competencies: Mastering Competitive Value from the Outside in, McGraw Hill, New York. S. 27-53.

Whitehurst, J. (2015). Open Organization, Harvard Business Review Press, Boston.

Wilson, T.D. & Brekke, N. (1994). Mental contamination and mental correction: unwanted influences on judgment and evaluations, Psychological Bulletin, 116:117-142.

Williamson, O.E. (2013). The Transaction Cost Economics

Project: The Theory and Practice of Governance and Contractual Relations, Edward Elgar Publishing, New York.

Winstanley, D. & Woodall, J. (2000). The Ethical Dimension of Human Resource Management, Human Resource Management Journal, 10, 2:5-20.

Winter, S.G. (2003). Understanding Dynamic Capabilities, Strategic Management Journal, 24:991-995.

Wittek, R.; Snijders, T. & Nee, V. (2013). The handbook of rational choice social research, Sage, London.

Wolfe, W.M. (2008). Winning the war of words, Praeger, London.

Womack, J.P. (2003). Lean Thinking: Banish waste and create waste in your corporation, Simon & Schuster, New York.

Wong, P.S.S. (2013). Drucker's knowledge-worker productivity theory, Lambert Academic Publishing, Saarbrücken, Germany.

Wright, P.M. & Boswell, W. (2002). Desegregating HRM: a review and synthesis of micro and macro human resource management research, Journal of Management, 28, 3:247-276.

Wright, P.M.; Boudreau, J.W.; Pace, D.A.; Libby Sartain, E.; McKinnon, P.; Antoine, R.L. (Eds.). (2011). The Chief HR Officer: Defining the New Role of Human Resource Leaders, Jossey-Bass, London.

Wright, P.M.; Gardner, T.M.; Moynihan, L.M. & Allen, M.R. (2005). The relationship between HR practices and firm performance: Examining causal order, Personnel Psychology, 58, 2:409-446.

Wright, P.M. & McMahan, G.C. (1992). Theoretical perspectives for strategic human resource management, Journal of Management, 18, 2:295-320.

Wright, P.M. & Nishii, L.H. (2013). Strategic HRM and Organizational behaviour: Integrating multiple levels of analysis, i Paauwe, J.; Guest, D.E. & Wright, P.M. (2013). HRM & Performance: Achievements & Challenges, Wiley, London. S. 97-110.

Wright, P.M. & Snell, S.A. (1998). Towards a unifying framework for exploring fit and flexibility in strategic human resource management, Academy of Management Review, 23:756-772.

Wright, P.; Dunford, B. & Snell, S. (2001). Human resources and the resource based view of the firm, Journal of Management, 27:701-721.

White, J. & Younger, J. (2013). The Global Perspective, in Ulrich, D.; Brockbank, W.; Younger, J. & Ulrich, M. (eds.); Global HR Competencies: Mastering Competitive Value from the Outside in, McGraw Hill, New York. S. 27-53.

Zhou, K.Z. & Bingxin, C. (2012). How Knowledge affect radical innovation, Strategic Management Journal, 33:1090-1102.

Zhou, Y.; Hong, Y. & Liu, J. (2013). Internal Commitment or External Collaboration? The Impact of Human Resource Management Systems on Firm Innovation and Performance, Human Resource Management, 52:263-288.

Zollo, M. & Winter, S.G. (2002). Deliberate learning and the evolution of Dynamic Capabilities, Organization Science, 13:339-351.

HRM-Visionarium

ABOUT THE AUTHOR

Jon-Arild Johannessen holds a Master of Science from Oslo University in History. He holds a Ph.D. from Stockholm University in Systemic thinking. He is currently professor (full) in Leadership, at Kristiania University College, Oslo and Nord University, Norway. He has been professor (full) in Innovation, at Syd-danske University, Denmark. He has been professor (full) in Management at The Arctic University, Norway. At Bodø Graduate School of Business, Norway he had a professorship (full) in Information management At Norwegian School of Management he has been professor in Knowledge Management.